Deva Victrix

Roman Chester
Re-assessed

Papers from a weekend conference held at
Chester College 3–5 September 1999

Supported by

Chester Archaeology

Edited by
PETER CARRINGTON
Chester 2002

ISBN 0 9507074 9 X

Abbreviations

The abbreviations used in this volume follow
the system laid down in BS 4148: 1985, as
recommended by the Council for British
Archaeology in Signposts for Archaeological
Publication ed 3, 1991, Appendix A

Notes for contributors

The Society welcomes articles about the
architecture, archaeology and history of
Cheshire in its Journal. If you are interested
in contributing, please contact the Editor at
the following address for further guidance on
the scope of the Journal and for notes on
style and layout:

Chester Archaeology
27 Grosvenor Street
Chester CH1 2DD
Tel: +44 (0)1244 402028
Fax: +44 (0)1244 347522

E-mail: p.carrington@chestercc.gov.uk

For more information about the Society, see:
http://www.chesterarchaeolsoc.org.uk

Designed and produced for the Society
by Aquarium Graphic Design 01244 398004

Foreword

The Chester Archaeological Society has a long tradition of producing publications of this sort. In the nineteenth century it initiated the debate on the date of Chester's walls. More recently it organised the conference which gave rise to the Rows Research Project. It was therefore appropriate that it should use the occasion of its 150th anniversary celebrations to refocus attention on Roman Chester, to see what all the work of the past generation or so amounted to and, just as important, where future priorities should lie.

It has to be admitted that the active role of the Society declined during the 1970s and 1980s — perhaps inevitably as the scale of 'rescue' fieldwork grew — and there are now other major players in the local archaeological arena, including a variety of commercial organisations as well as universities and local authorities. However, the Society has continued to fulfill an important function in keeping an independent and knowledgeable eye on the city's heritage and encouraging public appreciation of it. It is also now once again, especially through its fieldwork section, increasing the opportunities for local people to get involved in archaeology. Finally, as the conference that gave rise to this volume proves, it still has a role in initiating archaeological debates.

In recent years, proportionally the greatest advances have been made in our understanding of the archaeology of Saxon and medieval Chester, albeit bringing our knowledge of these periods from a very low base. However, it is concerning Roman Chester that most new data has been gained, and it is now time to summarise what has been learnt and begin to analyse and present it in the light of advances elsewhere. As we move out of the long shadows cast by the nineteenth-century European empires we are able to take a more detached view of the Roman world and apply more sophisticated approaches to its study. This volume represents a start in that direction, but there is a long way to go: it is to be hoped that future steps will be marked by contributions to the Society's journal.

The City Council's Archaeological Service is happy to have been associated with the conference and to support this publication. It recognises the value of the Society's civic role of constructive criticism and active participation and hopes that this volume will be the starting point for the open construction of a rolling research programme on Roman Chester.

It remains to thank the Society's Honorary Secretary, Dr David Mason, for his hard work in organizing the 1999 conference; Professor Bill Manning for his able chairmanship; the staff of Chester College for their hospitality; and the speakers for their lively contributions. Unfortunately this volume does not reflect the valuable contributions made by Dr Vivien Swan and Mr Tim Strickland, but relevant publications by them are noted below.[1]

G Storey, *Chairman, Chester Archaeological Society, 1998–2001*
M N Morris, *City Archaeologist*

[1] V G Swan, The Twentieth Legion and the history of the Antonine Wall reconsidered. *Proc Soc Antiq Scotland* **129**, 1999, 399–480;
T J Strickland, What sort of community existed at Chester during the hiatus of the second century? *In:* Goldsworth, A & Haynes, I eds. The Roman army as a community. (*J Roman Archaeol* suppl ser **34**, 1999), 105–10

Contents

Illustrations

Tables

I: Roman Fortress Studies
Present Trends and Future Questions

by Professor W H Manning PhD, FSA

Pre-Flavian legionary dispositions

By the early years of the second century AD the three legions stationed in Britain were in the fortresses where they were to remain until at least the end of the third century: Legion II *Augusta* at Isca (Caerleon), Legion VI *Victrix* at Eburacum (York), where it had replaced IX *Hispana*, probably at the beginning of Hadrian's reign, and Legion XX *Valeria Victrix* at Deva (Chester). All three were founded in the seventies of the first century AD. These fortresses have been known for centuries, but our knowledge of the legionary arrangements in the years before their foundation was less securely based and it is in that area that we have seen the greatest advances since the Second World War.

The position in the nineteen-thirties was stated by R G Collingwood in *Roman Britain and the English settlements* (Collingwood & Myres 1936). Collingwood was quite clear on the legionary arrangements which followed the invasion. After Camulodunum had fallen, the Roman army was divided into three columns which advanced from London. Legion IX struck north-east to Lincoln, where it established its fortress about 47; Legion II conquered the south and south-west of England, building a fortress at or near Exeter; while the third column, consisting of legions XIV and XX, advanced along Watling Street, first construct-ing a base in the High Cross area, south of Leicester, where Watling Street crosses the Fosse Way, and then moving on to found a double legionary fortress at Wroxeter. Probably before 50 Legion II was moved from Exeter to a new fortress at Gloucester. Unfortunately, as Collingwood admitted, there was no structural evidence for any of these fortresses, although in several cases tombstones confirmed that the respective legions had probably been based there at some time.

What is the situation today? The foundation dates of the Flavian fortresses remain unchanged, but later discoveries on the sites of Collingwood's postulated first fortresses only confirmed parts of his predictions. The fortresses at Lincoln and Gloucester were located soon after the Second World War, when development and excavation was resumed, but it was soon realised that neither had been built as early as the late forties; indeed the evidence suggests that Lincoln dates from the early sixties and Gloucester from the later sixties. At much the same time Aileen Fox found the fortress at Exeter, while Graham Webster's work at Wroxeter located the fortress there, although it was for a single legion, not the double fortress postulated by Collingwood. The corresponding fortress in south Wales was discovered in 1967 at Usk and shown, like Exeter and Wroxeter, to have been founded in the mid-fifties. Finally excavations in Colchester revealed that the *colonia* had been built on the site of a legionary fortress constructed immediately after the invasion.

What was surprising about these discoveries was that, except for Camulodunum, none of these fortresses had been built until the mid-fifties or later, some ten or more years after the invasion. Perhaps this should not have surprised us, for this was a time when the first phase of the conquest had been completed and the establishment of forward bases for the legions was a logical decision. If a name has to be given to the creator of this system, it must surely be that of Didius Gallus, governor from 52 to 57, and the construction of the fortresses at Exeter for Legion II, at Usk for Legion XX and at Wroxeter for Legion XIV can be seen both as the consolidation of his predecessors' conquests in western Britain and the necessary preparation for further advances in Wales and Cornwall. The fortress of Legion IX at Lincoln was built slightly later, in the early sixties, a fact which may be explained by the fact that unlike the western fortresses, which lay on frontiers where further military advances were imminent, the northern frontier was formed by the client kingdom of the Brigantes, and no campaign was envisaged against them at that time. Given its foundation date it is tempting to associate it with the suppression of the Boudiccan revolt of 60/61, which must have led to a major reconsideration of the military arrangements in eastern England.

However, the fact that most these fortresses had not been built until the mid-fifties raised the question of where the legions had been based before then. A possible solution was suggested by the discovery of a series of large forts, now usually called vexillation fortresses, ranging in size from around 4 to 10 hectares About fifteen are now known, and some ill-defined but extensive early Roman military sites such as that underlying Chichester probably fall into the same category. With the exception of Longthorpe we know little about the internal plans of these forts and we should not assume that all were of the same date, but they do provide an explanation for the missing early legionary fortresses. They suggest that for the first ten or more years of the conquest period most of the legions were split into smaller groups, possibly sharing their winter quarters and administrative centres with auxiliary troops — an arrangement which reflected the need to garrison the wide front on which the Roman army was operating in the later forties and early fifties. Only Legion XX at Colchester had a single base in the Claudian period, and that was probably as much for political as military reasons since Camulodunum was the *de facto* capital of the new province.

Fortress plans

It is unfortunate that we do not know more of the internal layouts and building plans of either the vexillation fortresses or the Neronian legionary fortresses, for the design of the legionary fortress was not static through the first century. The often unspoken assumption that the Flavian fortresses, as exemplified by Inchtuthil, were standardised, and that their predecessors were essentially of the same design, is disproved as soon as we look, for example, at the Augustan fortresses of Germany, which differed in important ways from their successors. To mention one example, their gates are of a type which we never find even in the Claudio–Neronian fortresses of Britain. Nor is there the uniformity of overall planning which is often claimed. Admittedly there is a high degree of standardisation in the types of buildings present but far less in where they should be placed within the fortress. Even rectangularity of plan was not sacrosanct.

Perhaps more surprisingly there are enormous gaps in our knowledge of the interiors of the Flavian fortresses. Very little is known of York, which was perhaps the most important of them all, and while the basic plans of Chester and Caerleon are fairly clear, much of the detail remains obscure. By contrast, we have the complete plan of Inchtuthil, even if it is one with rather a lot of dotted lines. But Inchtuthil was never completed and it is interesting to note the buildings which came at the end of the order of priorities: several tribunes' houses, the *praetorium* and, surprisingly, the main bath house. One of the most striking features of the plan is the small size of the *principia* and the fact that it lies in the middle of a large open space, both suggesting that the timber building was going to be replaced with a stone *principia* as soon as the first phase of construction was completed. This, together with the fact that a stone wall was inserted into the front of the fortress rampart, suggests that Inchtuthil was intended to have a degree of permanence which its pre-Flavian predecessors had lacked.

Questions for the future

Turning to the future, we may ask what questions remain. The answer is a lot: so many that only a few can be discussed here. One obvious need is to obtain more detailed knowledge of the overall plans and of the buildings within fortresses of all periods. A glance at the plan of any of them shows how woefully inadequate our knowledge actually is, and how lavish is the use of the broken line when overall plans are produced. One wonders to what extent the stone phases reflected their timber predecessors. We assume that they did, and indeed for the major buildings this seems likely, but we should remember the small *principia* at Inchtuthil, which would surely have been rebuilt in stone on a larger scale. The more or less complete excavation of a site to its lowest levels was rare before the nineteen-fifties, and how many key sites were excavated before then?

Another interesting question concerns the relationship between the legionaries and the inhabitants of the *canabae* around fortresses. Did these people have free access to the fortress? The finds from the baths at Caerleon suggest that they were used by women and children. We know that there were legal restrictions on the rights of legionaries to marry, but we also know that they often formed stable relationships with women during their service. This in turn raises the question of whether they always slept in their barracks or whether they lived, at least for part of the time, with their families in the *canabae*, where they must have owned or at least paid for their family's accommodation. A very large proportion of the people living in legionary *canabae* will have been related to the serving legionaries or have been discharged legionaries themselves, but the nature of their interaction with serving soldiers is ill-understood.

We know from literary sources that the legionary legates often had their families with them, and, given their high social status, they will have had large households, a fact which is confirmed by the enormous size of their houses. The Vindolanda tablets have revealed aspects of the social life of the wives of auxiliary commanders, and this must have applied on an even grander scale in legionary fortresses. Nor is there any reason to suppose that the junior officers did not bring their families with them: certainly they will have had slaves and servants. Within the fortress such households will have provided models of civilian life in a military context, and one wonders how they related to the rest of the fortress. At a lower social level, inscriptions make it clear that centurions and even ordinary legionaries often owned a slave, which raises the question of where they lived. It would have been highly inconvenient for a soldier if his personal slave had to spend most of his time outside the fortress.

Then there is the question of how the Roman army was supplied with its equipment and other necessities, as well as the luxuries which the men undoubtedly demanded and could afford. Here again we may have over-emphasised the difference between the military aspects of the fortress and the life of the civilians outside it. In his account of the temporary camps of the second century BC Polybius mentions the *forum* or market. There are no obvious market places inside the fortresses of the first century AD, but one may wonder if the market function died with the Republic. Are we correct in assuming that all commerce was confined to the *canabae*? Could some of the so-called *tabernae* which lined the roads at Inchtuthil really have been shops or even bars? One of the compounds which fronted the *via principalis* at Usk, in the position occupied by the *tabernae* at Inchtuthil, produced exceptionally large numbers of amphora stoppers, suggesting that the vessels were opened and their contents distributed there, but were those contents being sold or issued as rations? The enigmatic 'Elliptical Building' at Chester is not dissimilar in plan to certain *macella* found in Italy and the eastern provinces, which prompts the question of whether the resemblance could have extended to function as well as form. And who sold the mutton chops, pigs' trotters and chickens (head removed but feet still on) which the bathers gnawed in the *frigidarium* of the legionary baths at Caerleon?

In short, perhaps we should ask if legionary fortresses were not more open, more 'civilian', than we usually believe, with the inhabitants of the *canabae*, many of whom were related to past or present legionaries, normally free to wander in and out as the occasion required? The excavation of part of the *vicus* of the auxiliary fort at Vindolanda has shown how close this ran to the fort, in places almost touching its defences. Our knowledge of the *canabae* around legionary fortresses is very limited, but they must have been major settlements in their own right (those at York were raised to the status of a *colonia*, a status achieved by very few towns in Britain) and their relationship with the fortress at their core must have been both intimate and complex.

Turning to other matters. Many of the gaps in our understanding of how a legionary fortress functioned are due quite simply to our lack of detailed knowledge of the buildings involved, a lack which only major new excavations will resolve. For example, no complete legionary barrack block has been excavated in Britain since the nineteen-twenties, when many of the questions which we would ask today would not have been postulated and certainly could not have been answered. And hardly any major building — baths, *principia*, *praetorium*, workshop or hospital — have ever been completely excavated in a British fortress. Do we always have to wait until a developer threatens such a building before we can excavate it? And are we to postpone research excavations forever on the grounds that future techniques will always be better than those in current use — an argument which is becoming increasingly common.

A great deal of attention has been devoted to the origins of these fortresses, rather less to their later history. Among the reforms which remodelled the Roman world at the end of the third century was a major change in the status of the legion. With the creation of field armies, the legions were divided into units of around 1000 men and those units dispersed to various posts. This development is well known but its possible effect on the legionary fortresses has often been ignored. One result would have been that eighty percent of the barrack accommodation would have become redundant. The *praetorium*, built for a member of the senatorial order with a large staff and great wealth, will have passed to a man who was little more than a minor officer and who must have found such a vast palace impractical and inconvenient. And a whole series of enormous buildings, the *principia*, the workshops, the granaries and the baths, built to serve 5,000 men, were now used by one fifth of that number, and that fifth had to maintain them if they were to be retained. It seems unlikely that such a drastic reduction in manpower had no affect on the physical structure of the fortresses, but the archeological evidence for it remains obscure.

One problem which this reduction creates is in deciding when a fortress was actually abandoned. The evidence is clearest at Caerleon. The *Notitia Dignitatum* states that Rutupis, the Saxon Shore fort at Richborough in Kent, was under the command of the Prefect of the Second Augustan Legion. Clearly by the date of the *Notitia*, which is unlikely to have been compiled much before the end of the fourth century, the remnants of Legion II had been removed from Caerleon. In fact excavations there suggest that some of the major buildings, including the *basilica* of the *principia*, the baths and the hospital had been demolished before the end of the third century and that the amphitheatre was abandoned at much the same time. Given this, and the information in the *Notitia*, what is more obvious than to conclude that the fortress had been closed at that time and the reduced legion moved to Richborough? But can we assume that the abandonment of these great buildings really does mean the final closure of the fortress? Would it not have been logical for the reduced unit to have demolished some of the buildings which they had inherited and for which they can have had little use? The final answer may well be that the legion was completely removed, but the question remains — how do we differentiate between evidence of reduction and evidence of closure? To do so will require careful and extensive excavation of the later levels, which, inevitably, are those most likely to have been disturbed in the past and to which earlier excavators rarely devoted much time or effort.

One final point. In the nineteen-sixties the excavation of groups of barracks in some auxiliary forts on Hadrian's Wall revealed that they had been remodelled in the fourth century to convert them into rows of small individual dwellings, so-called 'chalet barracks'. Presumably these reflect the reduced size of the auxiliary garrisons of this period, perhaps even the introduction of soldiers' families into the forts. We now know that such barracks were normal in late Roman auxiliary forts in the north of England, but what of legionary barracks? Could some of those have been modified in the same way? Given the number of barrack blocks in a fortress it is clear that a fourth-century legion need have modified only a small proportion of the barracks, a fact which will not make their location any easier. None have been found as yet, but one has to remember that many of the auxiliary barracks which are now known to have been remodelled had already been excavated earlier in the twentieth century without this modification being recognised. Given the high proportion of legionary barrack blocks which were also excavated in the first few decades of the twentieth century, we may ask if there is any reason to suppose that excavators who failed to recognise them in auxiliary forts will have been more observant on legionary sites.

Further Reading

Boon, G C 1972 — Isca. The Roman legionary fortress at Caerleon, Mon. Cardiff: National Museum of Wales

Bowman, A K 1994 — Life and letters on the Roman frontier: Vindolanda and its people. London: British Museum

Brewer, R J ed 2000 — Roman fortresses and their legions. London: Society of Antiquaries/ Cardiff: National Museums and Galleries of Wales

Collingwood, R G & Myres, J N L 1936 — Roman Britain and the English settlements. Oxford: Clarendon Press. (Oxford History of England)

Crow, J 1995 — Housesteads. London: Batsford

Frere, S S 1987 — *Britannia*: a history of Roman Britain. London: Routledge & K P

Manning, W M 1981 — Report on the excavations at Usk: the fortress excavations 1968–1971. Cardiff: University of Wales Press

Manning, W H 1989 — Report on the excavations at Usk: the fortress excavations 1972–1974. Cardiff: University of Wales Press

Pitts, L F & St Joseph, J K 1985 — Inchtuthil: the Roman legionary fortress. London: Society for the Promotion of Roman Studies. (*Britannia* monogr ser **6**)

Webster, G ed 1988 — Fortress into city: the consolidation of Roman Britain, first century AD. London: Batsford

Zienkiewicz, J D 1986 — The legionary fortress baths at Caerleon. 2 vols. Cardiff: National Museum of Wales

II: The Exploration of Roman Chester 1962–1999
Retrospect and Prospect

by P Carrington PhD, FSA, MIFA

Introduction

This paper covers a period of almost forty years. In this time approximately fifty interventions have been carried out inside the Roman fortress and slightly fewer outside. They have ranged from small (including evaluations) to large. Even in those cases where the main purpose has not been to learn about the Romans, information about that period has generally been recovered

As well as reviewing the major interventions and the reasons for them, the objects of this paper are to review what we have learnt (ie advances in understanding as well as data) and, in particular, to suggest some topics that seem to be deserving of research in the future. References to some works that have appeared since the conference have been included.

Retrospect

The 1950s and the Richmond research agenda

There are two starting points for understanding post-war excavation in Chester. One is Sir Ian Richmond's research agenda; the other is the City Council's redevelopment schemes. In 1949, at the invitation of the Chester Archaeological Society, Richmond set out the following research priorities (Crosby 1999, 84–5):

- establish the precise line of the west wall of the fortress

- determine whether there was Roman occupation at Chester before the foundation of the Flavian legionary fortress

- establish whether turf and timber defences had preceded the stone defensive walls

- investigate crucial sites west of the Town Hall (then vacant as a result of slum clearance)

- establish the south-west corner of the fortress

- obtain information about Roman lifestyle in Chester, military and civilian

- opportunistic emergency excavation

These priorities may now seem very modest, but they were essentially practical ones, related to what was firmly known about Roman Chester at that time. For that, we may refer to Newstead's plan of 1948 (pl 1; here Ill II.1): the line of the fortress wall was accurately located in the north and east parts of the walled city, but that of the south and west defences was still conjectural; a number of barracks had been excavated in the Deanery Field; the outline of the *principia* had been roughly plotted but little was actually known about the building; the southern half of the 'Elliptical Building' had been uncovered, but its structural form was not understood, let alone its purpose; part of the *basilica* of the fortress baths was known, but not recognised for what it was; and there were a few minor structures.

Richmond's agenda was pursued so far as possible through the 1950s, first by Graham Webster and then by Hugh Thompson. Unfortunately, resources were never available for more than small-scale excavation, so although much was learnt about the defences little was done in the Town Hall area, where area excavation was required. By contrast, some 'rescue' opportunities were seized upon, for example to learn about the granaries. The fruits of this phase of research can be seen in the fortress plan in Thompson's *Roman Cheshire* (1965, plan facing 25; here Ill II.2): the lines of the defences had been firmed up; the *principia* more firmly delineated as a result of Webster and Richmond's Goss Street excavation of 1948/9; the *basilica* of the baths more accurately plotted, and the granaries and a few more barracks added. In addition, controlled extra-mural excavation had started, including the beginning of what was to be a ten-year programme on the northern half of the amphitheatre, and further afield there were a number of seasons on the neighbouring civilian site at Heronbridge. (For a summary of work in these years, *see* Crosby 1999, 84–7; Webster 1992–3; Thompson 1992–3, 50–3).

The 1960s onwards: city-centre redevelopment and large-scale rescue excavation

This comparatively leisurely advance changed in the 1960s with a number of development schemes: first the Inner Ring Road, which ran immediately alongside the western defences, then the Central Area Development Scheme, which encompassed the area around the Town Hall. Both of these schemes were Council-led. In addition the Grosvenor Shopping Centre was built over the south-eastern quarter of the fortress.

It was Dennis Petch, Curator of the Grosvenor Museum from 1963 to 1974, who had this challenge to face (*see* Petch 1992–3, 59–60, 63–4), and a preliminary attempt at plotting and interpreting the discoveries made in these years can be seen in his contribution to Jarrett's revision of Nash-Williams' *Roman Frontier in Wales* (Petch 1969, plan facing 36; here Ill II.3). Major advances can be seen in the area west and north of the *principia*: the First Cohort barracks, courtyard *fabrica*, Elliptical Building and '*praetorium*'; likewise in the south-eastern corner of the fortress the plan of the baths and the barracks to their east was recovered. As was the case elsewhere in the country, the pressures faced during this decade led to the establishment in 1972 of a dedicated field unit, initially constituted as the Excavations Section of the Grosvenor Museum and latterly as Chester Archaeology.

Large-scale excavation continued through the 1970s and early 1980s, although at a rather less hectic pace and far better resourced. The main gains of these years were in detailed knowledge of the barracks in the *retentura* and First Cohort areas and in the buildings

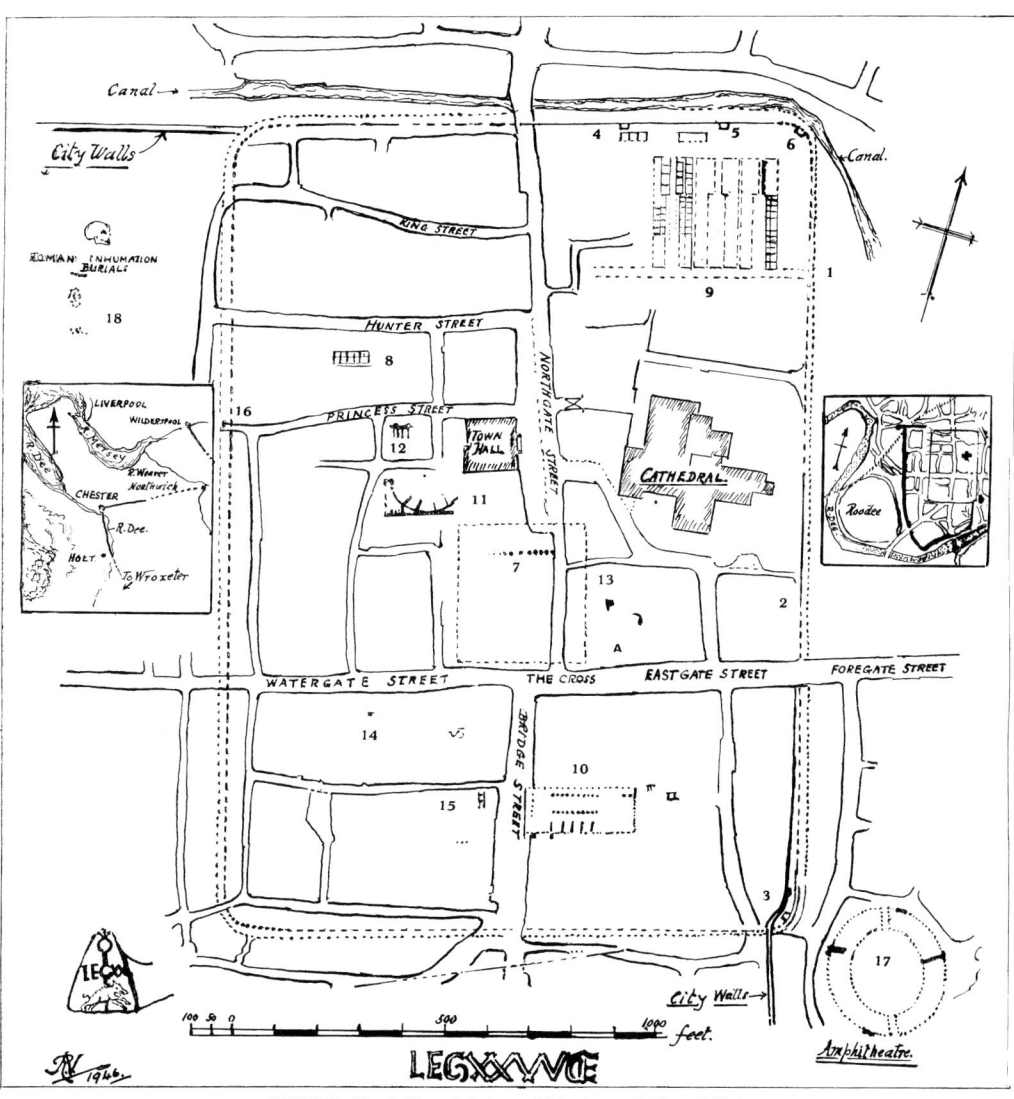

CHESTER (Deva)—Plan of Fortress. Dimensions *c.* 1,930 × 1,400 feet.
Red :—definite ; . . . conjectural.

KEY TO PLAN

SITE NO.	PAGE
1. Extra gateway to road in *Retentura* (Barrack blocks) Deanery Field (1935) ** - - -	2
2. Section of Fortress Wall (East) (1928) * - -	3
3. S.E. Angle of Fortress Wall and Angle Tower, etc. (1908, 1930) * - - - - -	4
4-6. Defensive Towers and buildings in *Intervallum* (1923—1935) ** - - - - -	4
7. Column Bases *Prætorium,* Northgate Street (1897) ✝ - - - - - - -	7
8. Barrack Buildings, Hunter Street (1909, 1914) *	8
9. Barrack Buildings, Deanery Field (1923—1935) **	9
10. Colonaded Building (Schola) St. Michael's Row (1863, 1908, 1926—7)‡ - - - -	11
11. Theatre-like Building (1939) ** - - -	13
12. Portion of Granary (1939) ** - - - -	13

SITE NO.	PAGE
13. Hypocaust, Northgate Street (1892) C. - -	14
A. Leaden Waterpipes, dated A.D. 79. Discovered 1899* - - - - - - - -	1
14. Column base, Watergate Street (1890) C. -	14
15. Column bases, Bridge Street (1899) * - -	14
16. Section of Defensive Ditch (W.) (1945) * and G.	3
17. Amphitheatre (1929—1934) ** - - - -	14
18. Burial Ground (Second century interments) (1912—1917) * - - - - - -	23

Those marked * explored by Professor R. Newstead.
„ „ ‡ „ by Professor R. Newstead.
(East and West portions only).
„ „ ** „ by Professors R. Newstead and J.P. Droop.
„ „ * G. „ by Professor R. Newstead and Mr. W. F. Grimes.
„ „ ✝ „ by Mr. H. Beswick.
„ „ C. „ Casual.

III II.1 Roman Chester: plan (after Newstead 1948, pl 1). (Not to scale)

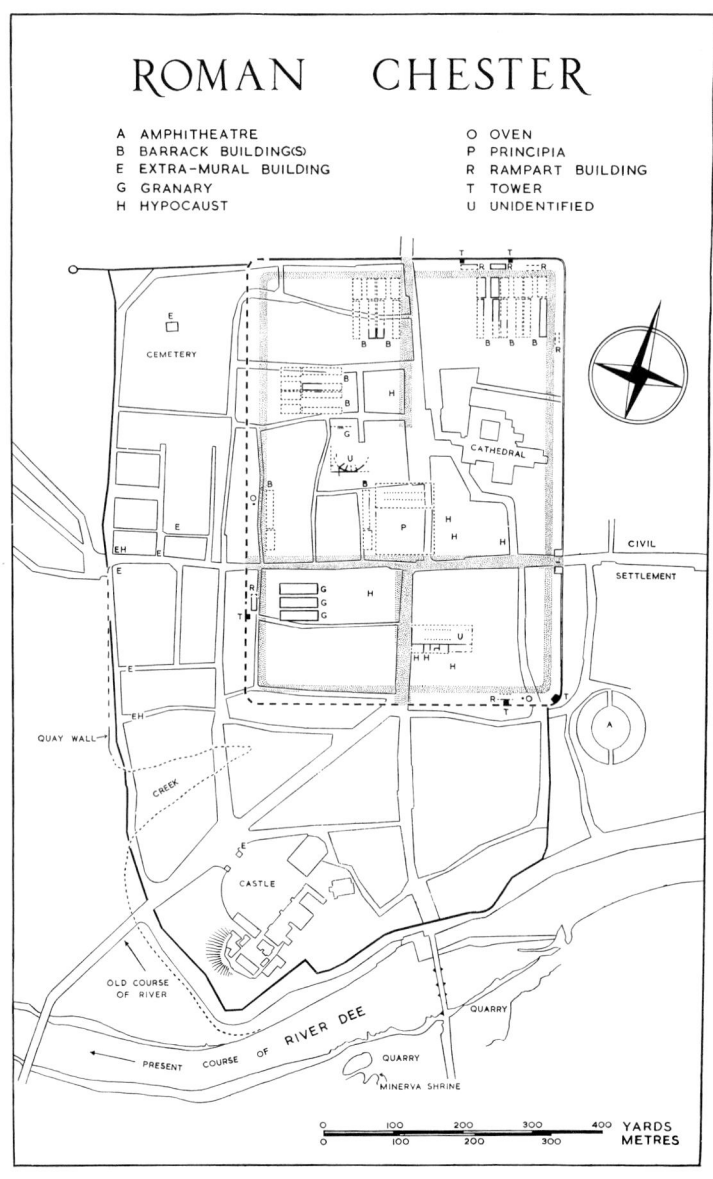

ROMAN CHESTER

A AMPHITHEATRE
B BARRACK BUILDING(S)
E EXTRA-MURAL BUILDING
G GRANARY
H HYPOCAUST

O OVEN
P PRINCIPIA
R RAMPART BUILDING
T TOWER
U UNIDENTIFIED

III II.2 Roman Chester: plan (after Thompson 1965, plan facing 25). (Scale 1/10,000).
(Copyright estate of F H Thompson)

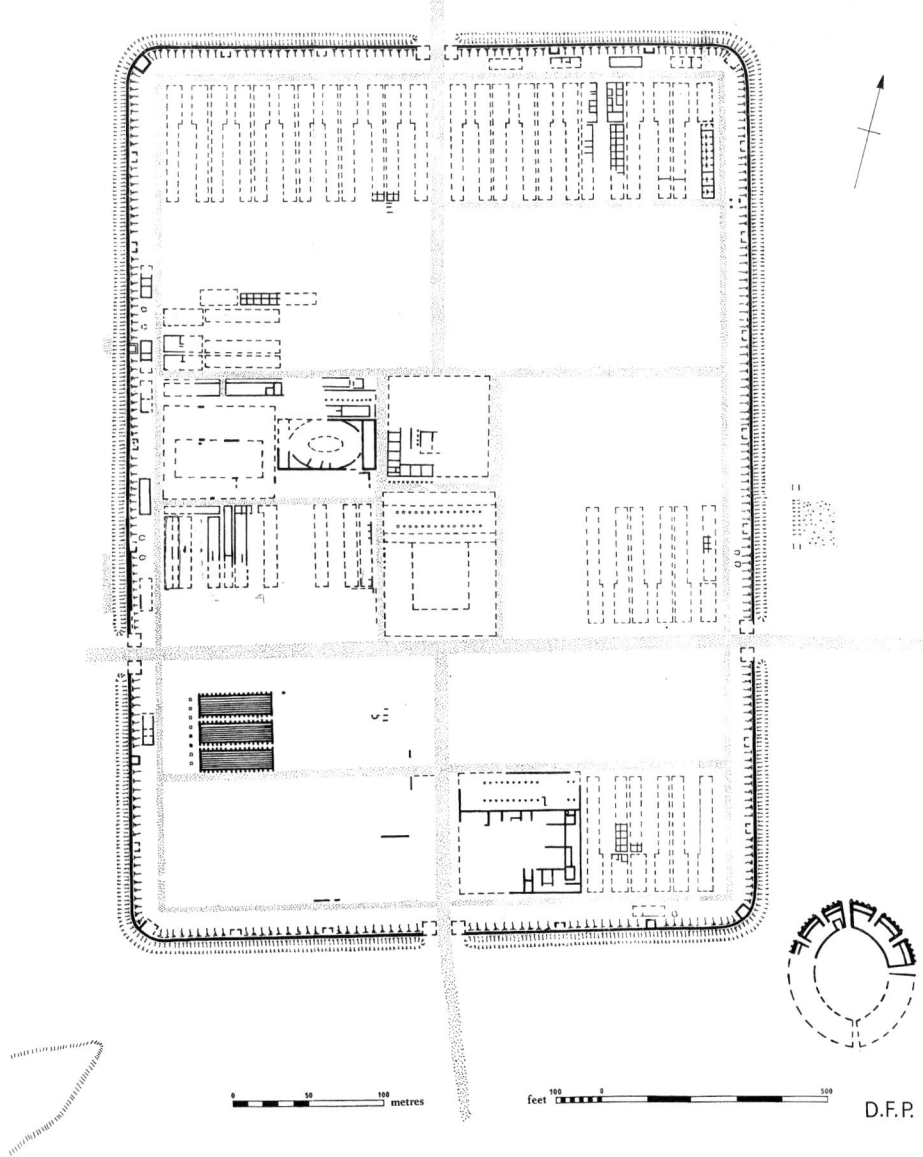

III II.3 Roman Chester: plan (after Petch 1969, plan facing 36). (Scale 1/5000).
(Copyright Chester City Council)

which lay to the north and north-west of the *principia*. These advances are shown in the fortress plan by David Mason (Ill II.4). The 1970s and 1980s also saw the first major excavations — with the exception of the amphitheatre — in the civilian settlement outside the fortress. Finally, closer links with the City's Conservation section were manifested in research on the City Walls (Strickland 1992–3, 87).

A number of major changes occurred in the 1990s. First, the study of the archaeology of periods other than Roman, which had been developing in Chester from the 1950s but particularly from the 1970s, gained much greater recognition. Secondly, the preservation ethic clearly expressed in PPG 16 drastically reduced the need for deep excavation in the city centre. Finally, the curator/contractor split led to Chester Archaeology withdrawing from most 'rescue' excavation in the city and district.

Thus, most fieldwork over the past forty years has been a logical continuation of the original Richmond agenda, seeking to plug basic gaps in the fortress plan and to start to fill the void outside it. A more selective approach, just looking for evidence to answer specific, sophisticated questions, as is now fashionable, would have been irresponsible. As a result we now have a fairly comprehensively excavated fortress and enough data of all sorts to allow us to pose, and at least begin to answer, a very wide range of questions.

Publication

The excavations of the 1950s were small and few enough to be reported promptly in the Society's *Journal*, although not in the detail that one would now wish. This system collapsed under the weight of continuous, large-scale excavation in the 1960s. An English Heritage-funded 'backlog' post in the 1980s (occupied by David Mason) prepared the ground for eventual full publication but was not adequate in itself to secure that objective. Fortunately the City Council has continued to accept the prime responsibility for post-excavation and publication, and a series of reports is now heading towards publication (Morris 1992–3, 98).

Because of the increasingly varied demands on staff time, especially for outreach work, the rate of publication remains frustratingly slow, despite contracting out large pieces of work, and much information is still only available in archive. In addition, it has to be remembered that there have been many post-Roman discoveries which have been equally worthy of seeing the light. We could have produced summary reports of many excavations a decade ago: indeed, some urged us to do so. However, it is likely that the result would have been that detailed publication would effectively have dropped off the agenda for the foreseeable future, and the full value would consequently not have been gained from the fieldwork that was carried out against such odds in the 1960s.

The approach taken to publication has been flexible. All recent reports have been monographs: some have combined the results of a number of related investigations; others have focussed on a single large site. The first part of a two-part report on the defences, focussing on the conservation-led research of the 1980s, has now been published in partnership with Gifford & Partners (LeQuesne *et al* 1999). This will be followed by David Mason's report on the Elliptical Building, scheduled for winter 2000, then by his report on

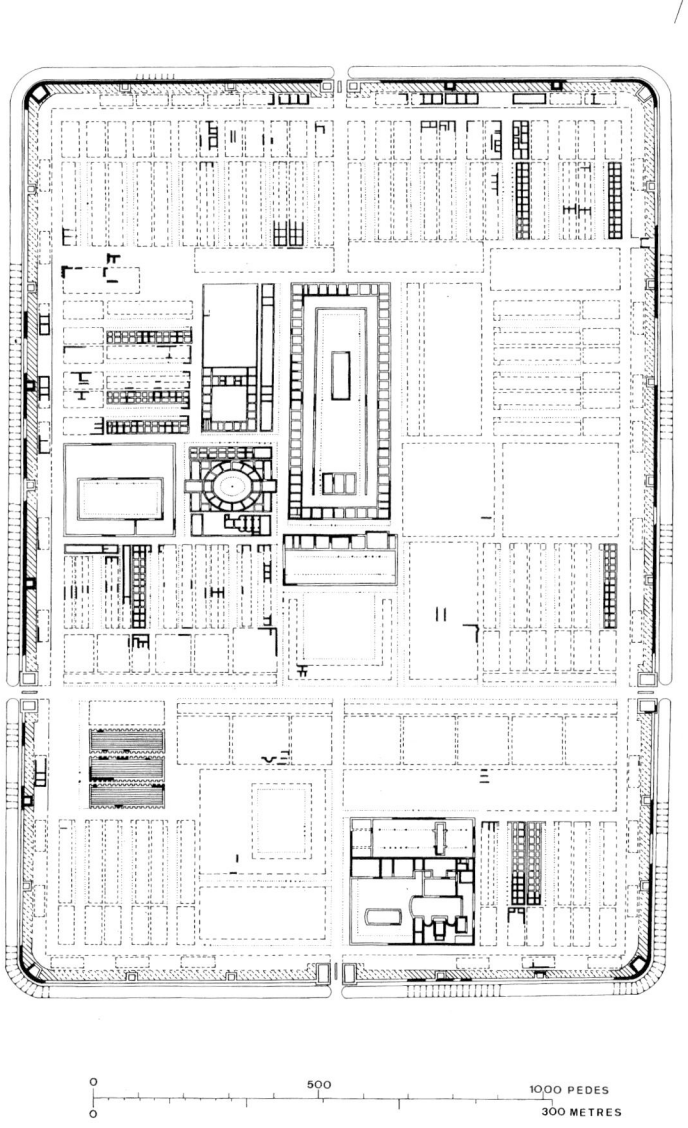

III II.4 Roman Chester *c* AD 230: plan (Mason 2000, 141, ill 98). (Scale 1/5000).
(Copyright D. Mason and Chester City Council)

the fortress baths (Mason 2000; *forthcoming*). A first report on the extra-mural area is at the editorial stage.

Review
Turning points
Over the past forty years we have unearthed much that we now know is fairly normal about Roman fortresses. What have we learned that is important or distinctive?

Chronological complexity and the 'military hiatus'
A multiplicity of timber phases was discovered during the excavation of a centurion's quarters at Northgate Brewery in 1974/5. The same site also produced evidence for a hiatus in occupation roughly corresponding to the building of the Hadrianic and Antonine walls and the Antonine occupation of Scotland, in all of which Legion XX VV was heavily involved (Ward & Strickland 1978, 19, 27). These discoveries introduced a degree of structural complexity and fluidity into the picture which, in retrospect, should always have been expected and which has been found on subsequent excavations and during re-examination of the archives of earlier ones.

The fortress plan
It is now accepted that the *praetorium* was not in its 'usual' place behind the *principia*. The building in that position was first uncovered by Dennis Petch in 1967–9. In his interim report (Petch 1968) he argued that the building he had excavated was the *praetorium*, but without much conviction. When more of what must be the same building came to light in 1979–82, the issue was settled (Strickland 1982, 16–22).

The fortress defences
Conservation work on the northern and eastern sectors of the City Walls from 1978 onwards gave opportunities to examine the stone defences. Until that time most archaeological research was directed at the southern and western defences, and thus at the rampart, given that most of the stonework there had been robbed centuries ago. LeQuesne's recent publication makes it clear that the stone 'wall' was, in fact, merely a facing supported by the rampart behind. The northern and western stone walls are thought to have been built at about the end of the first century, while a different foundation technique in the eastern and southern walls, backed up by a little artefactual dating, suggests third-century construction for those sectors. The availability of easily cut sandstone made it possible to build the wall in a monumental style from large blocks — an effect that elsewhere could often only be reproduced by covering a structure of small blockwork in stucco and painting on the 'joints'.

The Roman-Saxon interface
Although we had been routinely recognising late Saxon 'Chester ware' pottery in excavations since the early 1970s, understanding the accompanying stratigraphy was a problem until 1980. Then, in the Hunter's Walk excavation, we realised that this stratigraphy was represented by the post holes, other cut features and patchy surfaces immediately over the Roman; ie there was no intervening stratigraphy and no depth of late Saxon stratigraphy was to be expected. This discovery led to a general redating of features

assumed to be immediately post-Roman and enabled us to build up the picture of late Saxon Chester we have today (Ward *et al* 1994).

Parallel studies

Expanding knowledge of the fortress, coupled with research elsewhere, triggered a number of other debates:

The beginning and end of Roman occupation

The fairly complete stratigraphic sequence inside the defences at Abbey Green prompted thoughts about the beginning and end of the fortress: the former in the light of 'Steven's Urn' (Stevens 1942); the latter given the presence of obviously ancient roads and other features immediately over the Roman remains. Initial thoughts on these subjects were put forward in *New Evidence for Roman Chester* (McPeake 1978a; 1978b). These ideas have now been largely superseded but are still repeated. The strategic arguments relating to the foundation date for the Chester fortress in the context of the conquest of North Wales were reviewed by Carrington (1985a) and have stood the test of time better.

Metrology

Study of the metrology of the fortress, ie the units of measurement used in its surveying, began with trying to extrapolate the fragmentary remains found on the Northgate Brewery site and led to extensive comparisons with the overall plans of other fortresses throughout the empire (Ward & Strickland 1978, 27–8; Carrington 1985b; 1986). This is a subject where it is difficult to get clear-cut results at the best of times, and especially so without the use of large-scale plans.

The same comparison of fortress plans made it clear that there may have been an additional *scamnum* (building strip) in the *praetentura* between the tribunes' houses and the baths which, on the analogy of Neuss, might have been occupied by auxiliaries (Carrington 1985b, 38).

Artefactual studies

The outline of the pattern of pottery supply to the fortress was characterised (Carrington 1977, 147–8, 158–9; Ward & Carrington 1981).

The *canabae* and *prata legionis*

The relationship between the fortress and its immediate hinterland has received little study. One exception is David Mason's study of the legionary *prata* — the territory assigned to the legion so that it could feed itself — as a spin-off from his doctoral thesis (Mason 1986).

Current and future research

The strengthening of the 'preservation ethic' has led to a decline in large-scale excavation in the city centre. Conversely the potential for reassessment of old discoveries has been appreciated (Morris 1992–3, 102), sometimes in association with improved interpretation of sites or with fresh, small-scale fieldwork. Even so, large-scale excavation still has a contribution to make. Below are some examples of major outstanding questions which could be tackled using various of these techniques. Some of these questions are traditional, 'factual' ones; others concern the interpretation of data to shed light on behavioural issues (*see* James & Millett eds 2001, *passim*).

The fortress

The beginning and end of Roman occupation

As indicated above, the start of military occupation at Chester is still uncertain. In addition to the arguments about Chester in the context of North Wales, new ideas have emerged concerning early Roman contacts overland with the western Brigantes in the 50 and 60s of the first century AD (*see* especially Rogers 1996). Theories about operations in the two theatres — North Wales and Lancashire — need to be reconciled. In both cases a base at Chester for naval operations in support of land campaigns remains possible (eg Shotter 1993, 4; 1994, 26; 2000, 36–8). In addition, a possible vexillation fortress founded in the early 70s was suggested by Hartley (1981, 245). Hints of two phases of 'pre-fortress' occupation have been now been detected by David Mason during his re-examination of the archive of the Elliptical Building and other structures in the central area (Mason 2000, 8–12). The end of occupation at Chester is also unclear. Coins virtually cease by 360–370. But was fourth-century occupation military or, as some have suggested, civilian? We also need to be on the look out for the effects of the reduction in the strength of the legions (*see* Manning and Hoffmann, *this volume*). At both ends of the chronological spectrum useful progress could probably be made by the detailed re-study of existing material, especially coins, pottery and small finds, the re-examination of stratigraphic records and a consideration of Chester in its regional context.

The fortress plan

Which buildings occupied the blank spaces on the fortress plan? It is a reasonable conjecture that the *praetorium* lay in the *insula* east of the *principia* (Carrington 1985b, 44; Matthews *et al* 1995, 5–6). Where, then, was the hospital — behind the *praetorium* (under the Cathedral), as at Inchtuthil, or on the *via praetoria* opposite the baths (Carrington 1986, 10–16)? Part of the latter site has already been excavated and it is possible that more will ultimately become available as a result of redevelopment. Was there indeed an additional narrow *scamnum* in the *praetentura*; if so, was it occupied by auxiliary barracks, as has been conjectured? Finally, which buildings occupied the *insula* on the east side of the present Town Hall Square? These are examples of important questions to which the answer is most likely to come from large-scale excavation.

Chronology of the fortress defences

Is the chronology of the stone defences put forward by LeQuesne correct? Mason (2000, 87) has argued interestingly that the foundation technique found in the eastern and southern defences is typical of Flavian work in Chester and that the rebuilding of this sector in stone therefore precedes that of the northern and western defences. This is not simply a chronological question but affects how one sees the intended status of the fortress (*see below*, 'Strategic function').

Architectural decoration

The 'Roman Gardens' were laid out just after the Second World War. Over the years many architectural fragments from the fortress have been deposited there, but documentation of their origins is often lacking. In advance of redisplay and improved access by the City Council in 2000, the Chester Archaeological Society systematically recorded all the stones. Subsequent steps would be to work out which buildings they came from and their dates and analyse their stylistic affinities.

The canabae

Our data about the civilian settlement immediately outside the fortress has increased considerably as a result of fresh excavation since it was last summarised by Mason (1987; but *see* now this volume). One detailed report, dealing with discoveries to the west of the fortress, is at the editorial stage as a Chester Archaeology monograph, and there is material for another two volumes. However, at the moment these are merely descriptive accounts: what is needed to supplement them is a well founded synthesis dealing with wider questions of overall plan, chronology and function.

Watergate Street baths

Even on the level of individual buildings there are still major gaps to be filled. Remains of the Watergate Street baths, seen on a number occasions and tentatively suggested to be part of a legate's palace, could profit from a detailed report (Mason 1987, 146–9; 2000, 95 and 97, note 19).

The amphitheatre

The excavation of half of the amphitheatre in the 1960s was a major achievement. However, a rapid survey of the exposed structure, together with the excavation records and finds archive, has suggested that major re-interpretation of the building, its chronology and function may be necessary. For example: were the 'timber' and 'stone' phases at least partly contemporary? Is the masonry associated with the 'box' over the east entrance Roman at all? Does the recognition of occasional human remains affect the 'sanitised' view that the main function of the amphitheatre was for military training and display? On a more theoretical level, what was the role of the amphitheatre in social relations in Roman Chester as a whole? Chester Archaeology have drawn up a detailed research design covering these and other questions and in summer 2000 carried out small-scale excavations with the support of English Heritage which confirmed that even the excavated part of the site still had research potential.

The port and trade

The harbour installations are poorly known and are an example of a topic where archive re-assessment, in this case of nineteenth-century discoveries in the vicinity of the so-called 'Roman quay wall', could be profitably combined with small-scale excavation to explore the structure (Mason, *this volume*).

The contents and nature of the 'trade' that must have gone on through Chester's port in Roman times has received little attention. We may safely infer that, after coming up the estuary, lead ingots from Halkyn were transhipped at Chester (where one appears to have fallen overboard) for forwarding by road (Carrington 1984/5, 103). Some types of pottery vessels (or, more accurately, their contents) were almost certainly imported by sea, for example amphorae. On the other hand, some ubiquitous wares, eg Black-burnished I from

Dorset, could have arrived by sea or land, and it may not be possible to decide which. With others, such as Severn Valley ware, both modes of transport may have been employed (Carrington 1977, 153–5). Conversely, there will have been exports to coastal or estuarine military sites in North Wales and north-west England (for example the Cheshire sandstone reported by Wheeler (1923, 102–3) from Caernarfon (Segontium). Further afield Roman objects have been reported from the promontory site at Drumanagh, north of Dublin (*Sunday Times* 21 January 1996), and it would be surprising if Chester were not involved in any trade between Britain and Ireland. It would be fascinating to see these finds published in detail to allow a search for parallels with Chester and Cheshire material. Of course, we know even less about the 'invisible' exports and imports that must have passed through the port. Working from both earlier and later periods, it would be reasonable to expect imports of cattle and slaves and the export of salt (Griffiths in Ward *et al* 1994,124). The problem would be finding archaeological correlates to confirm or deny these ideas. Although the port of Deva would certainly have been the most important on the Dee, we must remember that in the pre-Roman Iron Age Meols seems to have had a role in international trade (Matthews 1996, 12–14) and continued to function through the Roman period: what was the relationship between the two sites? Finally we must discard fixed notions of modern mercantile trade in favour of a variety of exchange mechanisms (Matthews 1996, 18–19).

Artefactual and environmental studies
Pottery
The scope for major advances in artefactual and environmental studies is vast and their implications possibly far-reaching, especially in understanding personal and group identities and processes of acculturation (eg Allason-Jones 2001; Hill 2001), as well as manufacture and trade.

To take just a few examples. In broad terms the earliest Roman pottery from Chester is typically Flavian in its forms and fabrics. However, one gets the impressions of numerous detailed variations in these characteristics, suggesting a number of small-scale suppliers with diverse backgrounds rather than the fairly uniform 'in-house' production one might expect of a long-established legion stationed in a ceramically backward area. Is this a result of the first garrison having been Legion II *Adiutrix*, newly raised from the Ravenna fleet and lacking any potters amongst its tradesmen? Or is the answer more radical? Shotter (1998–9, 46–8) has pointed to the relatively low value of coin losses at Chester at this time (in terms of *as*-value per coin). Is the answer that a significant part of the Chester garrison was actually made up of auxiliaries during these years? A first stage in studying this question would be to characterise the forms and fabrics in question in detail on an inter-site basis to confirm the apparent variety and then to consider parallels both for the forms and the overall phenomenon.

Holt
This leads on to the subject of Holt. Apart from the puzzle of its siting (a river-crossing on an early invasion route into North Wales?), the accepted dating for its main phase of operation — late 80s to 130s in broad terms — leaves a number of questions unanswered. What was the source of the ceramic materials for the earliest permanent fortress buildings,

for example the baths? Was there a later phase of pottery production, responsible for the African forms recognised by Mrs Swan? And what of the sources of building materials found at Chester but not so far at Holt, such as the 'Jupiter Ammon' antefixes, tiles stamped with consular dates, and *tubuli*? Again, a research design covering these questions has been prepared by Chester Archaeology (Jones & Carrington 1997), and a lot could be achieved by archive study.

Environmental remains

Data on animal bone from the Roman fortress has been accumulating since the late 1970s, but there are as yet few large groups (those from the Abbey Green 1975–8 and Hunter Street School 1979–81 excavations are noteworthy) and none of these have so far been published. We know that remains of the usual domesticated animals (cattle, pig, sheep) are present, but element representation needs further study to determine where animals were butchered. We also know little about kill-off patterns and thus about management for meat, hides, wool, milk and traction. Can we infer distinctive social strata or practices (eg feasting) or the preferences of the different elements of an ethnically diverse community from food debris? Exotica might also tell us about the former distribution of species or importation for a variety of reasons.

The position with other environmental evidence is even worse: as a naturally dry site perched on a sandstone ridge the Chester fortress generally appears to preserve such material poorly, although pollen samples from the northern turf rampart have given an indication of the vegetation cover at the time of the foundation of the fortress (Greig in LeQuesne *et al* 1999, 75–7) and quantities of charred grain were found during the 1989 Priory Place excavation in the eastern *canabae*. In addition, there are waterlogged conditions in parts of the eastern *canabae*. These have high potential for the preservation of plant macrofossils, including species that are unlikely to survive through charring, giving further indications of diet and local vegetation.

Finally, we must remember that Roman Chester as a whole was a quasi-urban 'consumer' site, and that to get a picture of the 'producer' side we must look further afield at smaller settlements in the area, for example for information on crops, animal husbandry and woodland management. Although this is especially true for environmental information, it is true for artefactual as well.

The prata legionis, Heronbridge and beyond

The first two of these subjects have been exhaustively reviewed by David Mason (1986; 1988b). He has suggested that the *prata* (the land attributed to the legion to meet its agricultural needs, possibly via tenant farmers) were confined to the east of the Dee and extended from Tarvin to encompass some or all of the Wirral. This is a subject for which there is no direct evidence (eg boundary inscriptions) and for which disputable indirect archaeological correlates have to be sought. On the west bank of the Dee, 2 km from the fortress and possibly just outside the *prata*, lay the roadside settlement of Heronbridge. This consisted of typical Roman commercial strip buildings and flourished from the late first to the late third centuries. Metalworking seems to have been a prominent activity. Mason has identified a pattern of 'civilian settlements' (*Zivil Dörfer*) near many legionary fortresses yet distinct from the *canabae* immediately outside the latter and has suggested that they owed their existence to the proximity of a fortress but a different administrative regime from the *canabae* (1988a). The Romanised style of the settlement at Heronbridge suggests that this difference was a not a crude distinction between Roman and 'native' or citizen and non-citizen. One naturally nowadays thinks in terms of the possibility of less regulated trade. The site has been investigated in a piecemeal fashion since 1929, and the planned excavations by the Society, combined with archive study, would put our knowledge of it on a much firmer footing.

Looking further afield, we need to know far more about all aspects of local rural settlements. Valuable work has been done by Collens (1994), Philpott (2000) and Nevell and others (Nevell ed 1998). However, fresh fieldwork can still spring surprises, as in the discovery of a new site near Tarporley, in advance of the laying of a gas pipeline. In contrast to most other local rural sites, this seems to have been relatively rich in artefacts.

Overview: strategic intention and cultural reality

Was the Chester fortress intended to have a particular function in the province, different in kind from those to be served by Caerleon and York, or were all three fortresses intended to play more or less identical roles in their respective geographical areas? We have now passed the stage of noting the obvious standardisation of Roman military sites and have begun to analyse the detailed differences. For example, in the case of auxiliary forts — partly because we are dealing with a relatively large number of small, extensively excavated sites — we have begun to classify the variations in plan and to infer the type of units that occupied them and can therefore speculate about their precise military role. However, because of their smaller number and greater size — and the consequent difficulty of excavating large parts of their interiors — little comparable progress has been made with the permanent legionary fortresses: a fortress is still just a fortress. David Mason has made a start by suggesting that the Flavian fortress was intended as a quasi-provincial capital (Mason 2000, 91–5; *this volume*), but this idea has yet to be subjected to critical appraisal. Moreover, this leaves the role of the Severan fortress still to be considered, for instance in the light of the function of the large courtyard building behind the *principia* and other buildings in the *latera praetorii*.

Roman military bases, as well as cities and villas, must have served as powerful cultural statements by the occupying power. The fortress at Chester began as a self-aware community of Roman — and at least superficially Romanised — citizens and their dependents among a population on the north-western limits of the empire with very different ways (James 2001). As time went by, the difference between 'Roman' and 'native' would have become blurred with local recruitment and veteran settlement. In addition, as one of the places where, at least until the mid-third century, a large proportion of imperial taxation was disbursed, it had a key role in the monetary cycle that sustained and unified the society of the 'High Empire', while the decline of that cycle was at the heart of subsequent changes (Hopkins 1980). If we look beneath the surface, we will see that the culture of the legionaries would always have been far from uniform, with periodic drafts from different parts of the empire. Perhaps in contrast to this *mischkultur* we can picture a more uniform Mediterranean 'high culture' among the legate and tribunes. Thus Chester must have exemplified the cultural trajectory of the empire in miniature. If we can grasp the essence of the archaeological topics listed above, then perhaps we can begin to appreciate the importance of the place.

Bibliography

Allason-Jones, L 2001 Material culture and identity. *In*: James & Millett eds, 19–25

Anderson, A C & Anderson, A S eds 1981 Roman pottery research in Britain and north-west Europe: papers presented to Graham Webster. Oxford: British Archaeological Reports. (BAR Int Ser **123**)

Carrington, P 1977 Severn valley ware and its place in the Roman pottery supply at Chester: a preliminary assessment. *In*: Dore, J & Greene, K T eds. Roman pottery studies in Britain and beyond: papers presented to John Gillam July 1977. Oxford: British Archaeological Reports. (BAR Suppl Ser **30**), 147–62

Carrington, P 1984/5 The eariest evidence for lead mining in Flintshire. *Cheshire Archaeol Bull* **10**, 102–5

Carrington, P 1985a The Roman advance into the north-western midlands before AD 71. *J Chester Archaeol Soc* new ser **68**, 5–22

Carrington, P 1985b The plan of the legionary fortress at Chester: a reconsideration. *J Chester Archaeol Soc* new ser **68**, 23–51

Carrington, P 1986 The plan of the legionary fortress at Chester: further comparisons. *J Chester Archaeol Soc* new ser **69**, 7–17

Collens, J 1994 Recent discoveries from the air in Cheshire. *In*: Carrington, P ed. From flints to flowerpots: current research in the Dee–Mersey region. Papers from a seminar held at Chester, February 1994. Chester City Council. (Archaeol Serv Occas Pap **2**), 19–25

Crosby, A G 1999 The Chester Archaeological Society: the first one hundred and fifty years 1849–1999. Chester Archaeological Society

Hartley, B R 1981 The early Roman military occupation of Lincoln and Chester. *In*: Anderson & Anderson eds, 239–45

Hill, J D 2001 Romanisation, gender and class: recent approaches to identity in Britain and their possible consequences. *In*: James & Millett eds, 12–18

Hopkins, K 1980 Taxes and trade in the Roman empire (200BC–AD 400). *J Roman Stud* **70**, 101–25

James, S 2001 Soldiers and civilians: identity and interaction in Roman Britain. *In*: James & Millett eds, 77–89

James, S & Millett, M eds 2001 Britons and Romans: advancing the archaeological agenda. York: Council for British Archaeology. (CBA Res Rep **125**)

Jones, A & Carrington, P 1997 Holt research project: draft research design. Unpubl report, Chester Archaeology

LeQuesne, C *et al* 1999 Excavations at Chester, the Roman and later defences, part I: investigations 1978–1990. Chester City Council. (Chester Archaeol Excav Surv Rep **11**)

McPeake, J C 1978a The first century AD. *In*: Strickland & Davey eds, 9–16

McPeake, J C 1978b   The end of the affair. *In*: Strickland & Davey eds, 41–4

Mason, D J P 1986   The *prata legionis* at Chester. *J Chester Archaeol Soc* new ser **69**, 19–43

Mason D J P 1987   Chester: the *canabae legionis*. *Britannia* **18**, 143–68

Mason, D J P 1988a   The Roman site at Heronbridge, near Chester, Cheshire: aspects of civilian settlement in the vicinity of legionary fortresses in Britain and beyond. *Archaeol J* **145**, 123–57

Mason, D J P 1988b   *Prata legionis* in Britain. *Britannia* **19**, 163–89

Mason, D J P 2000   Excavations at Chester, the Elliptical Building: an image of the Roman world? Excavations in 1939 and 1963–9. Chester City Council. (Chester Archaeol Excav Surv Rep **12**)

Mason, D J P *forthcoming*   Excavations at Chester, the baths of the Roman fortress: investigations 1732–1988. Chester City Council. (Chester Archaeol Excav Surv Rep **13**)

Matthews, K J *et al* 1995   Excavations at Chester, the evolution of the heart of the city: investigations at 3–15 Eastgate Street 1990/1. Chester City Council. (Archaeol Serv Excav Surv Rep **8**)

Matthews, K J 1996   3: Iron-age sea-borne trade in Liverpool Bay. *In*: Carrington, P ed. 'Where Deva spreads her wizard stream'. Trade and the port of Chester: papers from a seminar held at Chester, November 1995. Chester City Council. (Chester Archaeol Occas Pap **3**), 12–23

Morris, M N 1992–3   The future of Chester's past: 1989–96. *J Chester Archaeol Soc* new ser **72**, 95–107

Nevell, M ed 1998   Living on the edge of empire, models, methodology & marginality. Late-prehistoric and Romano-British rural settlement in north-west England. *Archaeol North-West* **3**(13)

Newstead, R [1948]   The Roman occupation of Chester (DEVA). Chester: Griffith

Petch, D F 1968   The *praetorium* at Deva. *J Chester Archaeol Soc* new ser **55**, 1–5

Petch, D F 1969   Chester. *In*: Nash-Williams, V E. The Roman frontier in Wales. Ed 2, revd Jarrett, M G. Cardiff: University of Wales, 33–42

Petch, D F 1992–3   Filling the gaps — a decade of growth: 1962–73. *J Chester Archaeol Soc* new ser **72**, 57–72

Philpott, R A 2000   The Romano-British sites in their regional context. *In*: Cowell, R W & Philpott, R A. Prehistoric, Romano-British and medieval settlement in lowland north-west England: archaeological excavations along the A5300 road corridor in Merseyside. Liverpool: National Museums & Galleries on Merseyside, 175–204

Rogers, I 1996   The conquest of Brigantia and the development of the Roman road system in the north-west. *Britannia* **27**, 365–8

Shotter, D C A 1993   Coin-loss and the Roman occupation of north-west England. *British Numis J* **63**, 1–19

Shotter, D C A 1994   Rome and the Brigantes: early hostilities. *Trans Cumberland Westmorland Antiq Archaeol Soc* **94**, 21–34

Shotter, D C A 1998–9   III: Chester, the evidence of Roman coin loss. *J Chester Archaeol Soc* new ser **75**, 33–50

Shotter, D C A 2000   The Roman conquest of the north-west. *Trans Cumberland Westmorland Antiq Archaeol Soc* **100**, 33–53

Stevens, C E 1942   Notes on Roman Chester. *J Chester Archaeol Soc* new ser **35** (1), 49–52

Strickland, T J 1982   Chester: excavations in the Princess Street/Hunter Street area, 1978–1982: a first report on discoveries of the Roman period. *J Chester Archaeol Soc* new ser **65**, 5–24

Strickland, T J 1992–3 Archaeology at the crossroads: 1973–89 – interesting pastime or sober profession. *J Chester Archaeol Soc* new ser **72**, 73–93

Strickland, T J & Davey, P J eds 1978   New evidence for Roman Chester. Liverpool University

Thompson, F H 1965   Roman Chester. Chester: Cheshire Community Council. (History of Cheshire **1**)

Thompson, F H 1992–3 The education of an archaeologist in a time of change: 1955–62. *J Chester Archaeol Soc* new ser **72**, 49–56

Ward, M & Carrington, P 1981   A quantitative study of the pottery from a Roman extra-mural building at Chester. *In*: Anderson & Anderson eds, 25–38.

Ward, S W & Strickland, T J 1978   Excavations at Chester, Northgate Brewery 1974/5: a Roman centurion's quarters and barrack. Chester City Council. (Grosvenor Mus Archaeol Excav Surv Rep **1**)

Ward, S W et al 1994   Excavations at Chester, Saxon occupation within the Roman fortress: sites excavated 1978–1981. Chester City Council. (Archaeol Serv Excav Surv Rep **7**)

Webster, G 1992–3   Reflections on archaeology and the creation of the Grosvenor Museum: 1948–5. *J Chester Archaeol Soc* new ser **72**, 37–47

Wheeler, R E M 1923   Segontium and the Roman occupation of Wales. (*Y Cymmrodor* **33**)

III: Chester

Early Roman Occupation

by D C A Shotter PhD, FSA

I t has been demonstrated that the evidence of Roman coin loss can make a significant contribution to our understanding of the pattern of military conquest and occupation in north-west England (Shotter 1993; 2000a). In particular it has proved possible, in cases where the coin sample is of sufficient size, to distinguish between sites whose initial establishment was pre-Agricolan, Agricolan, or post-Agricolan (Jones 1968; Shotter 2001). Over the years it has been postulated that Quintus Petillius Cerialis, Vespasian's son-in-law and governor of Britain from AD 71 to 74 (Birley 1973), may have made a greater impact on northern Britain than has traditionally been appreciated.

The purpose of the present paper is to develop further the arguments about early Roman military activity and, in particular, to examine the possible role of Chester in it. The pattern of Roman coin issue in the first century AD is especially helpful: the emperor Vespasian (AD 69–79) reorganised minting activities and, almost for the first time, ensured a supply of coins to meet demand. Pre-Flavian coinage, especially *aes* denominations, was more erratic in its appearance: in particular, local copying of the *aes* of Claudius was tolerated to ensure sufficient supplies, and such coins, which were often of poor quality (Sutherland 1937), circulated relatively freely in the reigns of Claudius and Nero, but are rarely found in assemblages of Flavian date. To a large extent, the same happened also to regular Julio-Claudian *aes* issues. The presence of such coins, therefore, becomes a guide to likely areas of pre-Flavian military activity. Further, Vespasian's reign saw two years of heavy coin issue, AD 71 and 77/8, and it seems reasonable to suppose that sites with a heavy representation of *aes* issues of 71 should be regarded *prima facie* as likely to have been established during the governorship of Petillius Cerialis.

A study of Roman coin loss in the north-west counties (Shotter 1994) has revealed that a considerable number of pre-Flavian *aes* issues has been retrieved from coastal and river valley locations and that Chester itself has yielded some (Ills III.1, 2). We know from the accounts of the Roman historian P Cornelius Tacitus (*Annals* XII, 31–40; *Histories* III, 45) that although Rome early on established a treaty relationship with Cartimandua of the Brigantes, factional squabbling in the 50s and 60s between her and her husband and rival Venutius threatened to destabilise the north-west; this culminated in the triumph of Venutius in 69, thus necessitating the 'rescue' of Cartimandua, perhaps from a centre at Barwick in Elmet (near Leeds; Carrington 1985). Tacitus makes it clear that such

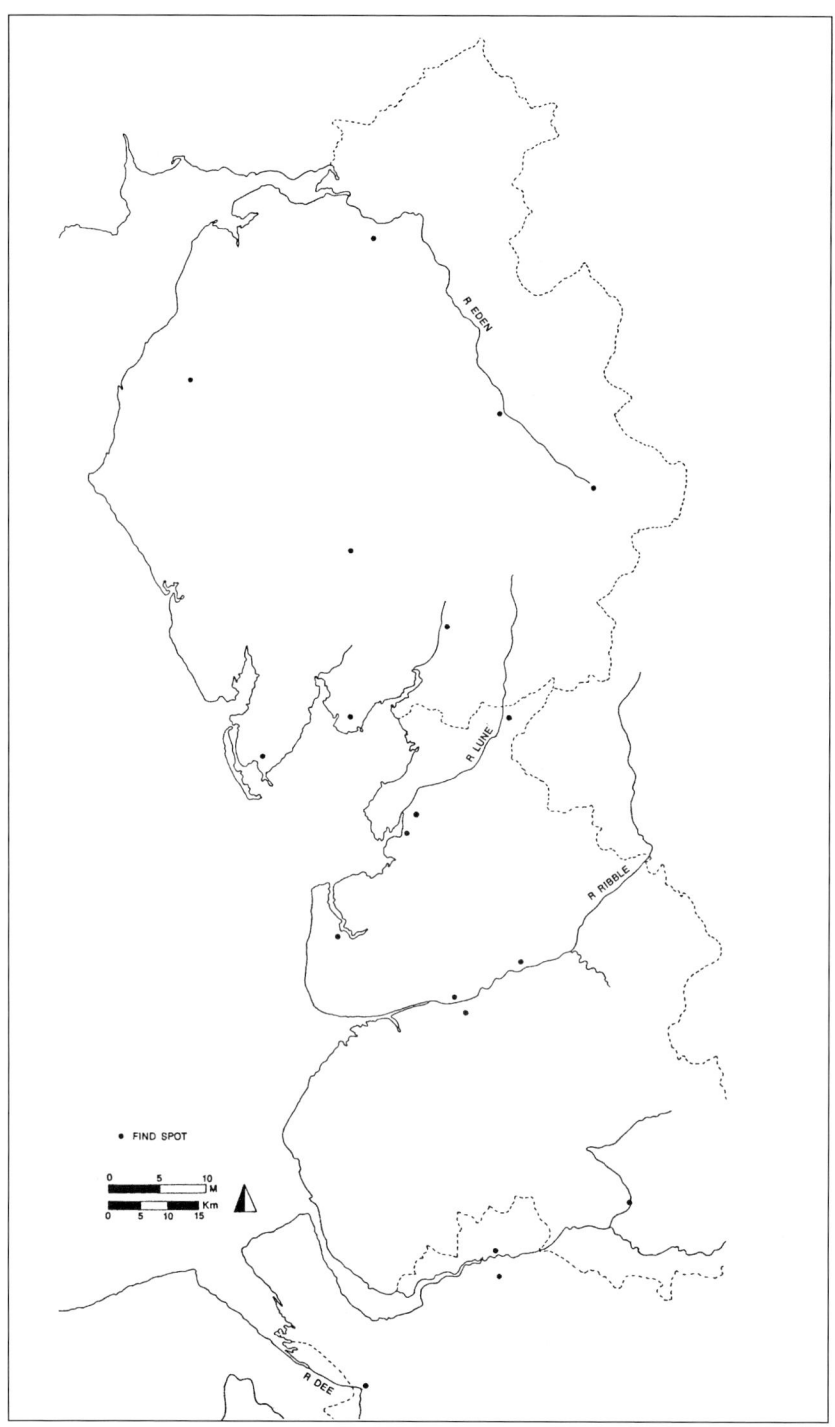

III III.1 Find spots of pre-Neronian *aes* coins: map.

squabbling necessitated a Roman response, which evidently came in the form of 'search-and-destroy' missions, but which did not lead at the time to permanent military occupation; the physical evidence of such activities, therefore, would have existed in the form of campaign camps which, on low ground at least, will have proved vulnerable to subsequent agricultural activity. However, sites such as Mastiles Lane (Malham Moor) might conceivably be relics of this period of campaigning.

The distribution of the early coin types described above suggests that the Roman army on these occasions set up 'combined operations' of a type evidently used again by Agricola in Scotland in the early 80s (Tacitus, *Agricola*, 25; Hanson 1987, 175). Troops worked overland from bases such as Wroxeter and Little Chester, penetrating into the north-west along the line of King Street through Middlewich, crossing the Mersey near Wilderspool, the Ribble at or near Walton-le-Dale, and making for Lancaster on the river Lune (Rogers 1996) (Ill III. 3). At the same time troops were probably shipped from the estuary of the Dee at or near Chester to be disembarked in the estuaries of the same rivers, where they would have joined up with their colleagues. The recent excavation of a complex of sites at Kirkham on the north bank of the Ribble estuary (Howard-Davis & Buxton 2000) lends weight to this, especially if access to Cartimandua's stronghold was gained along the Ribble–Aire corridor.

This re-opens the possibility of a 'pre-fortress' (and pre-Flavian) establishment at Chester, which has often been canvassed and discussed in the past (eg McPeake 1978); such a site, however, would probably have had a limited role. If the main route of penetration overland was represented by the line of King Street, then Chester lay at a considerable distance from it; further, marshy ground to the west of Chester will have left it as far from ideal for the overland penetration of north Wales. Indeed, it has been shown (Grew ed 1980, 365) that the road from the north-west midlands into north Wales originally crossed the Dee at Farndon/Holt (Jones 1991) and that its extension to Chester was a secondary development. Thus, it is likely that a role for Chester in these early days of conquest would have been tied to the movement of troops by sea along the coasts of north Wales and north-west

III III.2 Copies of *asses* of Claudius: (l) from Walton-le-Dale; (r) from Barrow in Furness.

England, although it should be kept in mind that such a role would have been of crucial importance.

As already indicated, the events of 69 had the effect of turning Brigantian territory into a hostile neighbour of the fledgling province of Britannia; the initial response to this must have been left to the incumbent governor, Marcus Vettius Bolanus, of whom Tacitus (*Agricola* 16,5) is decidedly — but probably unjustifiably — dismissive; references in classical authors, for example, leave open the possibility that Bolanus may have penetrated as far north as Scotland. Bolanus, however, was followed by a high-profile appointment — that of Petillius Cerialis who, according to Tacitus (*Agricola* 17,1), operated amongst the Brigantes, although the historian is decidedly short on detail. Recent examination of the coin evidence strongly suggests that Cerialis penetrated deep into Scotland, besides bringing much of Brigantian territory to heel (Shotter 2000b). Cerialis appears to have brought with him to Britain a new legion — II *Adiutrix* — which was of proven loyalty to the new emperor, Vespasian, to whom its soldiers (whilst still members of the fleet based at Ravenna in Italy) had deserted at a crucial point in the civil war of 69. These troops, therefore, were not only loyal to Vespasian but also were well acquainted with naval warfare. It would thus appear to have been a natural use of their talents if Cerialis had placed at least a detachment (*vexillatio*) of them at Chester to repeat the tactic, previously employed, of penetrating via the major river estuaries, perhaps on this occasion — in view of the now-proven presence of Cerialis at Carlisle — as far north as the Solway. Again, the coin evidence is consistent with the proposition of some activity at Chester in the early 70s. As before, other troops, such those of Legion XX, will have marched north from their bases in the north-west midlands (*see* Ills III.4, 5).

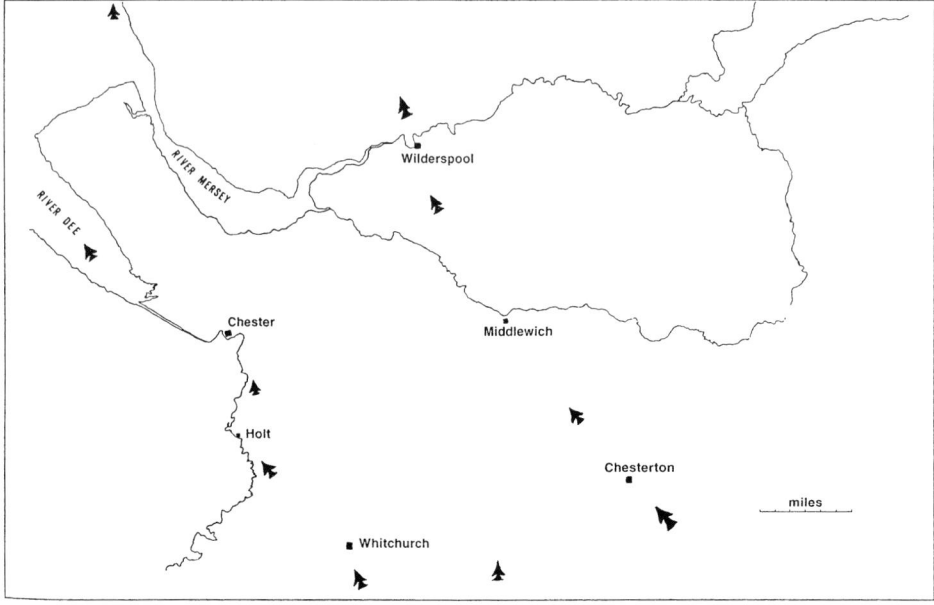

III III.3 Initial routes of military penetration into north-west England: map

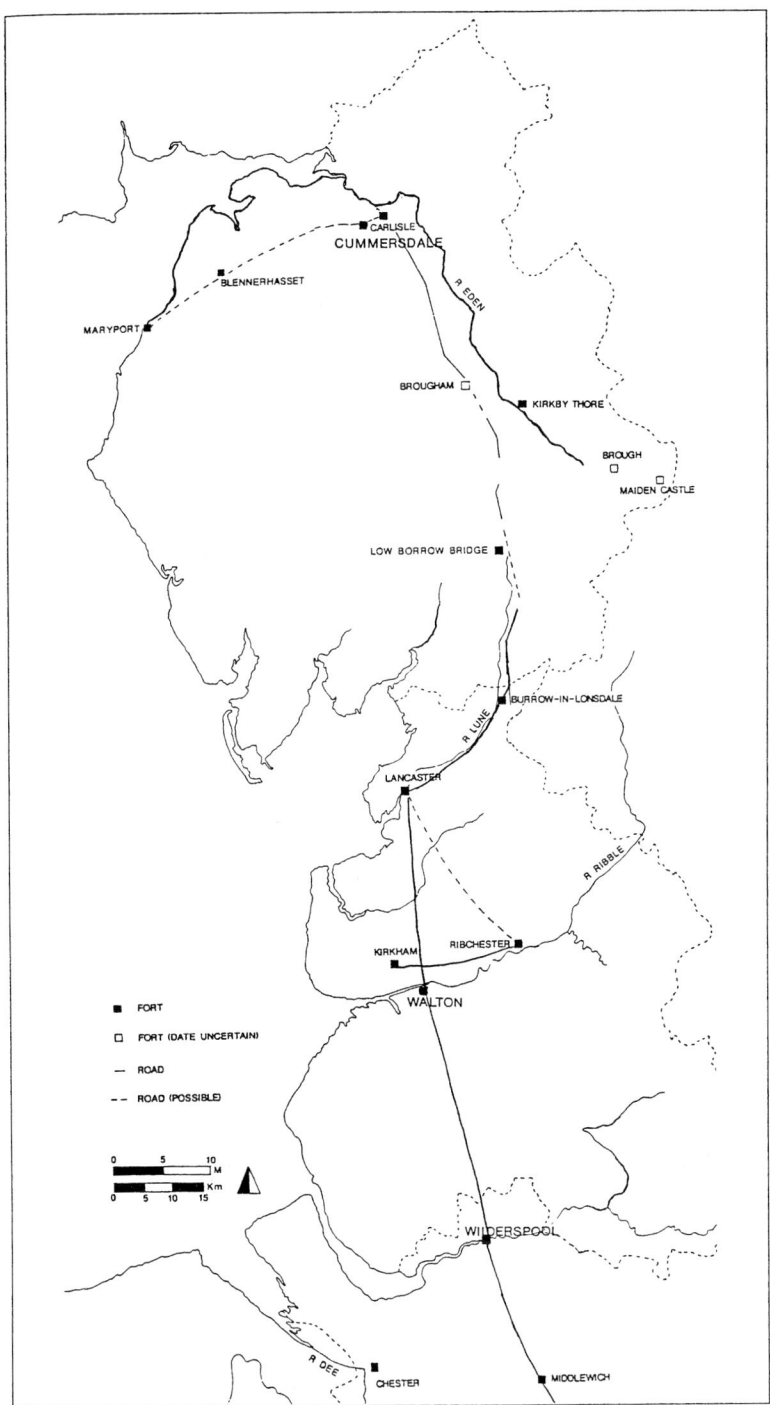

III III.4 Early Flavian sites in north-west England: map

Ill III.5 Southern gateway of the earliest fort at Carlisle: the well preserved timbers from this site provide a felling date of late in AD 72.

Thus, there would appear to have been a specific role in the early days of conquest for a site at Chester. However, once the conquest of the north was itself completed, the role of Chester changed, and, presumably, under Julius Frontinus (74–7) and Agricola (77–83), Chester received a new legionary fortress as a permanent base for Legion II *Adiutrix* and perhaps — as is suggested elsewhere in this volume — as a showpiece for the new Flavian dynasty. This new site received its own new routes of communication, through Northwich and Manchester to York and northwards to Ribchester and Carlisle (*see* Ill III.4). Whether a pre-fortress establishment, as is suggested here, lies beneath the known fortress or elsewhere in the area remains unclear, but the case for its existence seems powerful.

Bibliography

Birley, A R 1973 — Petillius Cerialis and the conquest of Brigantia. *Britannia* **4**, 179–90

Carrington, P 1985 — The Roman advance into the north-western midlands before AD 71. *J Chester Archaeol Soc* new **68**, 5–22

Grew, F O ed 1980 — Roman Britain in 1979, I. Sites explored. *Britannia* **11**, 346–402

Hanson, W S 1987 — Agricola and the conquest of the north. London: Batsford

Howard-Davis, C & Buxton, K 2000 — Roman forts in the Fylde; excavations at Dowbridge, Kirkham 1994. Lancaster University. (Centre for North-West Regional Studies)

Jones, G D B 1968 — The Romans in the north-west. *Northern Hist* **3**, 1–26

Jones, G D B 1991 — Farndon: an archaeological opportunity. *Manchester Archaeol Bull* **6**, 75–7

McPeake, J C 1978 — The first century AD. *In:* Strickland, T J & Davey, P J eds. New evidence for Roman Chester. Liverpool University, 9–16

Rogers, I 1996 — The conquest of Brigantia and the development of the Roman road system in the north-west. *Britannia* **27**, 365–8

Shotter, D C A 1993 — Coin loss and the Roman occupation of north-west England. *British Numis J* **63**, 1–19

Shotter, D C A 1994 — Rome and the Brigantes: early hostilities. *Trans Cumberland Westmorland Antiq Archaeol Soc* ser 2, **94**, 21–34

Shotter, D C A 2000a — The Roman conquest of the north-west. *Trans Cumberland Westmorland Antiq Archaeol Soc* ser 2, **100**, 33–53

Shotter, D C A 2000b — Petillius Cerialis in northern Britain. *Northern Hist* **36**, 189–98

Shotter, D C A 2001 — 'Agricolan' is an overworked adjective. *In:* Higham, N J ed. The archaeology of the Roman empire: a tribute to the life and work of Professor Barri Jones. Oxford: British Archaeological Reports. (BAR Int ser **940**), 75–83

Sutherland, C H V 1937 — Coinage and currency in Roman Britain. Oxford U P

IV: The Foundation of the Legionary Fortress
Deva, The Flavians and Imperial Symbolism

by D J P Mason PhD, FSA, MIFA

Occasions such as this afford the opportunity to put forward new ideas and hypotheses and sometimes, metaphorically speaking, to 'put the cat among the pigeons'. The vast amount of new information produced by excavations during the last thirty years, in combination with the ongoing analysis of unpublished investigations conducted earlier, means that at last we can not only discern much of the fortress plan but can also actually reconstruct much of its internal layout at various phases in its long history, including that of the original fortress (Ill IV.1). The installation of a legion at Chester was part of the redeployment of the legions in Britain which took place in the 70s of the first century following the enlargement of the Roman province by the conquest of Brigantia. It is known from a fragmentary inscription that the main internal bath building (*thermae*) had already been completed by the middle of AD 79 at the latest. Given the time needed to construct this large and technically sophisticated building, it is probable that the lead ingots found at Chester datable to 74 mark the beginning of work on the construction of the fortress.

The question of whether there was Roman military occupation at Chester before the establishment of the legionary fortress has been much debated over the years, and in a resumé of recent work on Roman Chester published in 1978 (*New Evidence for Roman Chester*) the impression was given that the defences of a pre-Flavian fort or fortress and one of its internal buildings had been found on the Abbey Green and Goss Street sites respectively (McPeake 1978). However, reassessment of the evidence from both sites as a preliminary to publication has overturned this initial interpretation. The earliest building at Goss Street is now placed in the primary stage of the legionary fortress, while the collection of features at Abbey Green once viewed as a box rampart seem far more likely to have belonged to structures sited at the rear of the fortress rampart.

However, the analysis for publication of the archive of a site excavated even earlier has, paradoxically, yielded incontestable evidence of pre-fortress Roman military activity. The site in question lies at the heart of the fortress and was occupied by the so-called Elliptical Building excavated in the 1960s, of which more in a moment, a structure securely dated to the early Flavian period by an inscribed lead water pipe datable to the first half of 79. Beneath its courtyard was found a 15-m-long flat-bottomed and steep-sided ditch, 4.25 m wide and 1.25 m deep, very reminiscent of the short length of ditch and accompanying

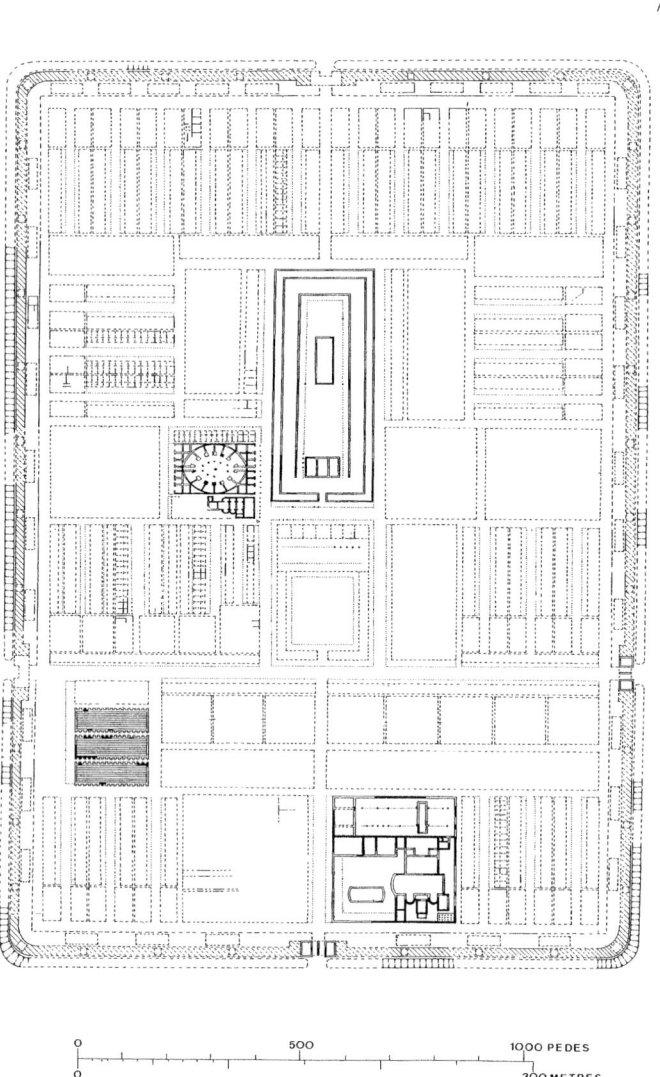

N

III IV.1 The primary fortress, *c* AD 75 plan. (Scale 1/5000)

| 0 | | | 500 | | 1000 PEDES |
| 0 | | | | | 300 METRES |

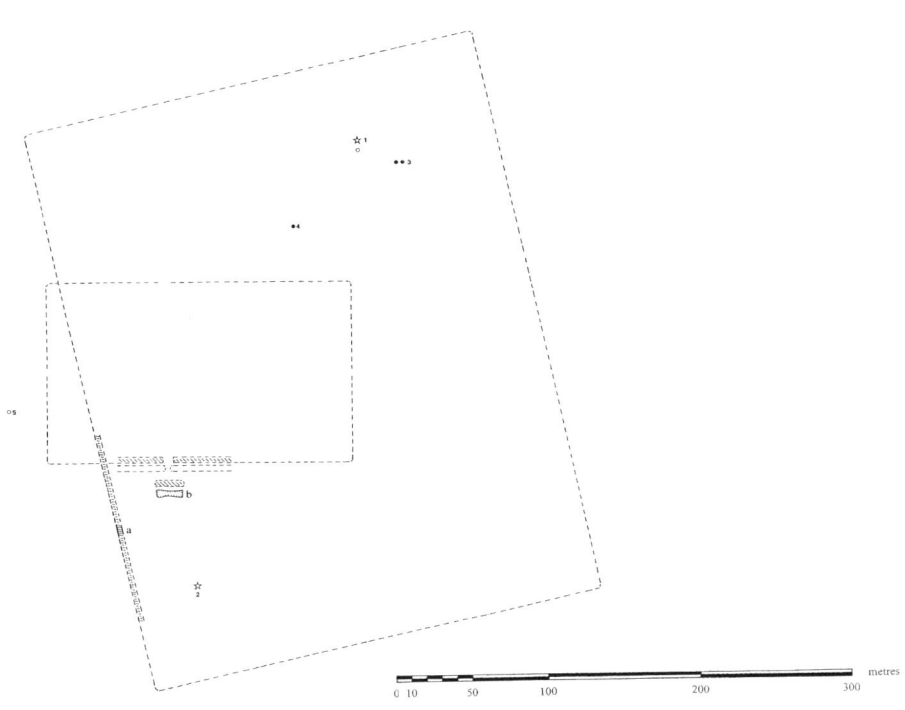

Ill IV.2 Pre-fortress ditch and other features beneath Elliptical Building: plan.
(Scale 1/5000). (Copyright D Mason and Chester City Council)

bank known as a *titulum* often provided as an additional defensive feature in front of the gates of Roman camps (Ill IV.2, b). Other early features were found beneath the south-west corner of the same building. These consisted of a foundation trench and a post pit belonging to a substantial timber structure (Ill IV. 2, a). This could have been a building or, just conceivably, a timber revetted rampart. Whichever, the most notable aspect of this structure is the fact that its alignment, south-east–north-west, is markedly different from that of all known phases of fortress buildings, and it is interesting to note that slight features following a similar alignment have been found underlying the earliest buildings on a number of sites within the fortress. While the restrictive conditions under which the 1960s investigations took place prevented detailed examination of the surrounding areas for further early features, there seems a strong possibility that the remains found below the Elliptical Building belong to at least one phase of pre-fortress, and perhaps pre-Flavian, Roman military activity at Chester.

Returning now to the legionary fortress, this was the usual 'playing card' shape and at 24.65 ha (60.90 acres) was the largest by far of the three fortresses constructed in Britain in the early 70s, York and Caerleon both being about 4 ha smaller. The reason why Chester needed to be 20% larger than its sister fortresses is unknown but a possible explanation is advanced below. The primary defences consisted of a 6-m-wide rampart with turf stack

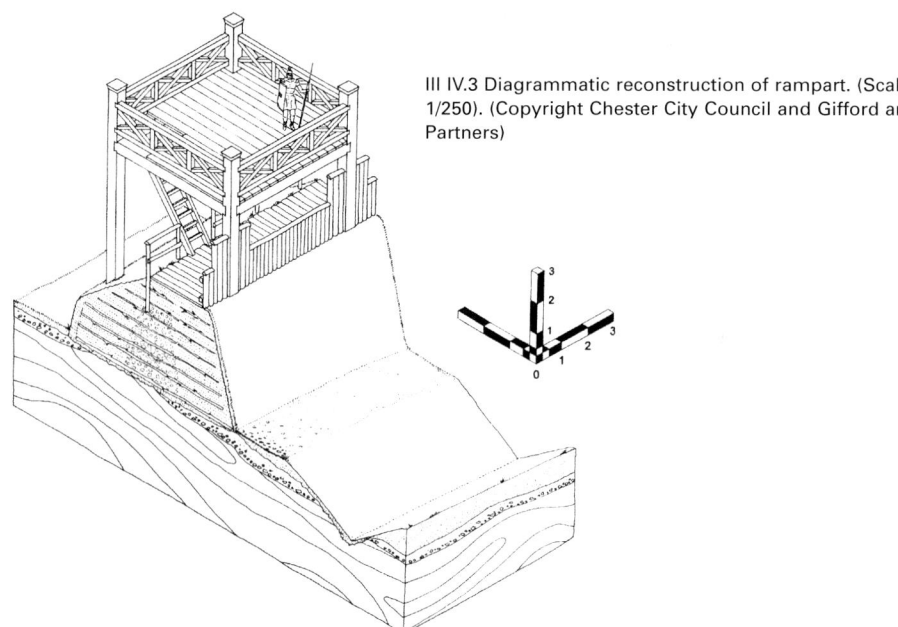

III IV.3 Diagrammatic reconstruction of rampart. (Scale 1/250). (Copyright Chester City Council and Gifford and Partners)

revetments front and rear enclosing a core of sand, clay and rubble with, as recent excavations have demonstrated, layers of logs and/or brushwood at regular vertical intervals of 1 Roman foot to provide structural reinforcement (Ill IV.3) The corner and interval towers — numbering thirty-six in all — were of timber, each raised on four principal posts. The earliest gateways were also undoubtedly of timber, but the discovery on the site of the south gate (*porta praetoria*) of a mass of very hard concrete of a type which only occurs in the Flavian period implies that a start was soon made on replacing these in stone. There are also hints that the provision of a masonry curtain wall with towers was begun soon after the foundation of the fortress. In front of the rampart and completing the defences was a single ditch approximately 3 m wide and 1.5 m deep.

The distribution of the internal buildings in their primary form is shown in Ill IV.1 and, apart from a few notable exceptions, these were constructed of timber. As usual, the accommodation for the ten cohorts of the legion was placed in the outer plots alongside the *via sagularis*, six barrack blocks per cohort of 480 men, with rather more for the First Cohort which had a complement of 800 or 960. Each barrack was 11.8 m wide and 83–84 m long overall, of which about 26.5 m was given over to the centurion's house (Ill IV.4). The portion of the barrack housing the ordinary legionaries was sub-divided into thirteen or fourteen *contubernia*. In addition to the barracks of two cohorts, the forward part of the fortress (*praetentura*) contained the houses of the senior officers. Although little explored, these probably fronted onto the main cross-street (*via principalis*), as in other fortresses. At the west end of this street, situated next to the *porta principalis dextra* so that grain brought by ship only had to be transported a short distance from the harbour, lay a group of three, or more probably four, stone granaries. Partly explored in the 1950s, additional information was recovered from an excavation in 1987. No trace of earlier timber buildings was found on either occasion and this, together with the fact that the stone buildings had foundations of hard cobble concrete typical of the early Flavian period, suggests that the stone granaries were among the few buildings of the early fortress to be built of masonry.

Another structure in the latter category was the main bath building of the fortress, lying beside the south gate (Ill IV.5). A sizeable portion of this building, consisting of a covered exercise hall of basilical form with a range of heated rooms equipped with mosaics along its south side, was exposed and subsequently destroyed by building works in 1863. Fortunately, a written, drawn and photographic record of the remains was made by Dr Thomas Brushfield, a prominent and distinguished member of the Society in its early days. Further discoveries at the east end of the hall followed in 1909/10 and 1926/7, including a chamber with a fine mosaic featuring a tableau of marine creatures (Ill IV.6). Another large portion of this complex was exposed, hastily investigated and then destroyed in 1963/4 during preparatory works for the

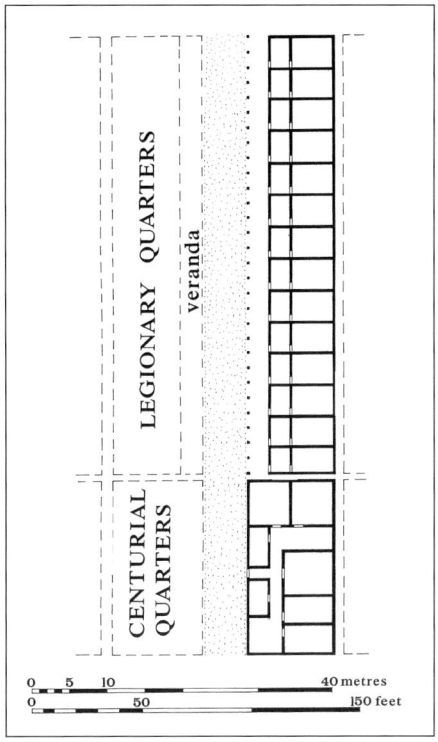

III IV.4 Layout of Flavian barracks: plan.
(Scale 1/1000)

construction of the Grosvenor Shopping Centre. This revealed that the room with the sea-creature mosaic was in fact the first of three large halls with vaulted ceilings (*frigidarium, tepidarium* and *caldarium*) which had formed the main bathing suite. Beyond the south end of the latter lay the principal furnace house with ancillary furnaces to either side, and beyond that again two large water reservoirs (*castella aquae*). The degree of preservation in this part of the complex was quite outstanding, with walls surviving to a height of 3.5 m or more and with hypocaust systems completely intact. The remaining quarter of the building to the south-west was occupied by an open-air exercise yard (*palaestra*), equipped with a large swimming pool. The fortress baths measured 85 m square overall and their completion during the reign of Vespasian is attested by a fragmentary inscription recovered from the exercise hall in 1863. The loss of this archaeological gem will be offset to some extent in the near future by the publication of a definitive report on this magnificent building based on analysis of the archive of information recorded in the 1960s along with all previous discoveries.

The plot opposite the baths has been little explored, and so the nature of the building(s) which stood there is unknown, although this is a likely position for the hospital. The remaining and largely unexplored space in the *praetentura* may have been used to accommodate a unit of auxiliary cavalry, as at Caerleon, but this is pure speculation. Occupying

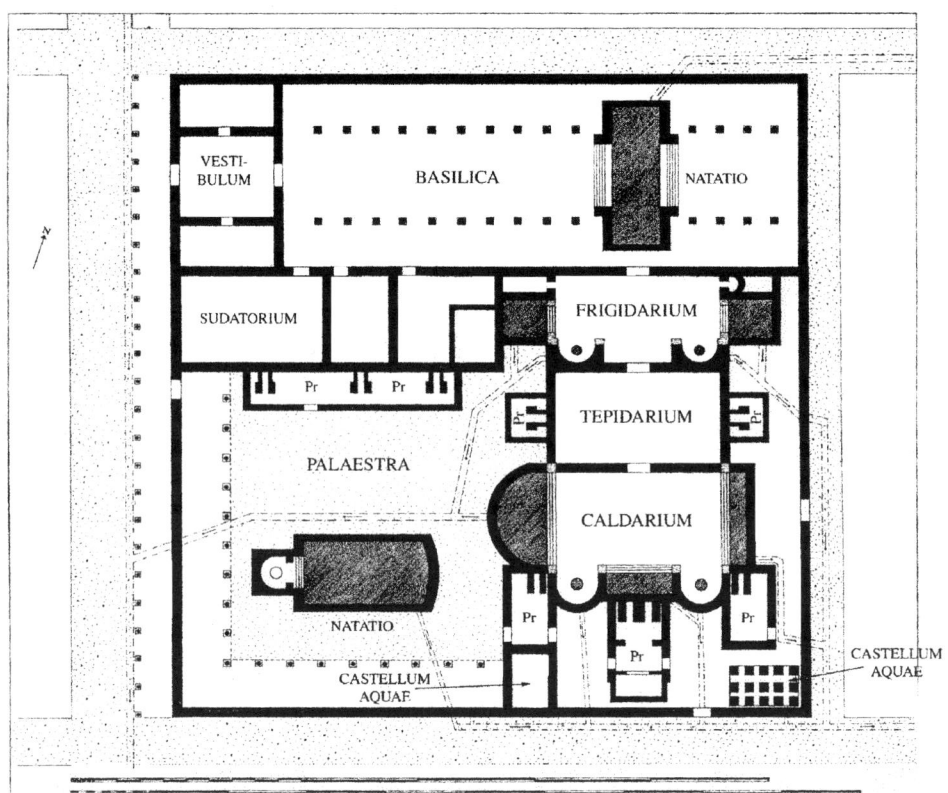

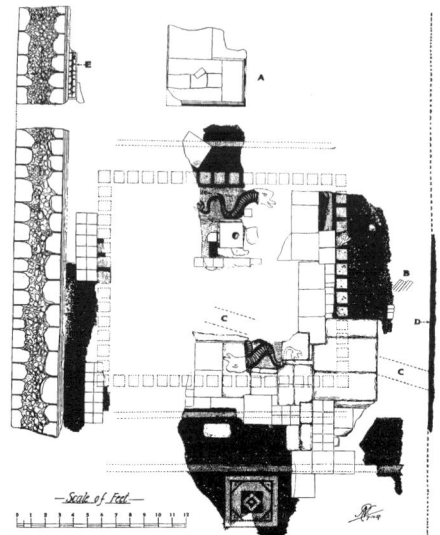

above: III IV.5 Flavian fortress baths: plan. (Scale 1/1000)

right: III IV.6 Drawing of marine-tableau mosaic floor, *frigidarium* of fortress baths, 1909/10. (Not to scale). (*J Chester Archaeol Soc*)

Plan of mosaic floor discovered 1909-10.
A. Platform? B. Tiles placed vertically downwards. C, C. Drain. D. South wall.
E. Buttress against North wall.

Site XXXVII. S. Michael's Row, p. 117.

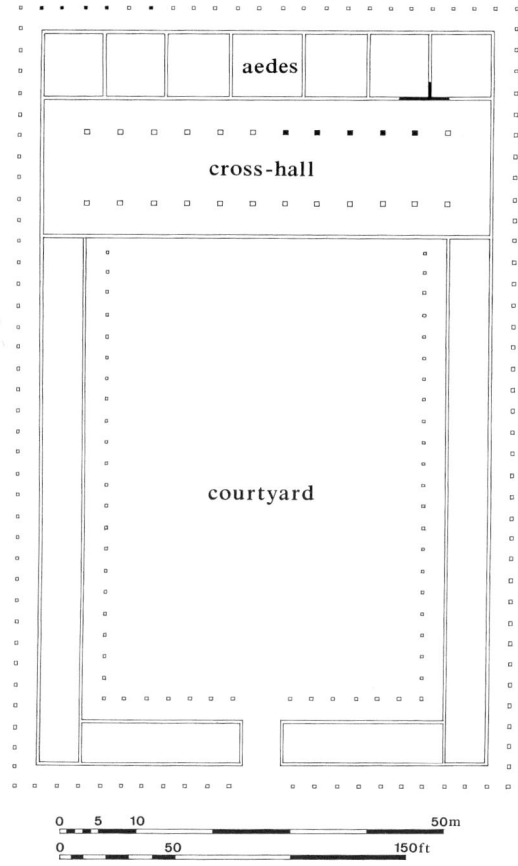

III IV.7 Primary timber headquarters building: plan. (Scale 1/1000)

its usual position at the junction of the *via principalis* with the *via praetoria* lay the head-quarters building (*principia*). Apart from a minor excavation close to its south-west corner, no other investigation of this building has occurred since the Old Market Hall and Goss Street excavations of 1969 and 1973 respectively. However, reappraisal of the evidence from the second of these as a prelude to publication has resulted in a new interpretation of the earliest phases (Ill IV.7). As a result the primary, timber, *principia* is now seen as having been *c* 8 m shorter in its east-west dimension than the fully developed third-century building, giving it an overall width of *c* 64.5 compared with *c* 73.15 m. As will be seen shortly, the legionary commander's residence (*praetorium*) at Chester did not occupy its normal position for this period, behind the *principia*, but instead, as had usually been the case in Neronian and earlier fortresses, took up the plot on its sinistral (east in our case) side. Little of this building has been examined methodically, although discoveries of hypocausts and mosaics many years ago attest the quality of its appointments.

It is the area at the centre of the rear half of the fortress which has been the scene of the greatest advances in knowledge. Two of the buildings here are rather unusual to say the

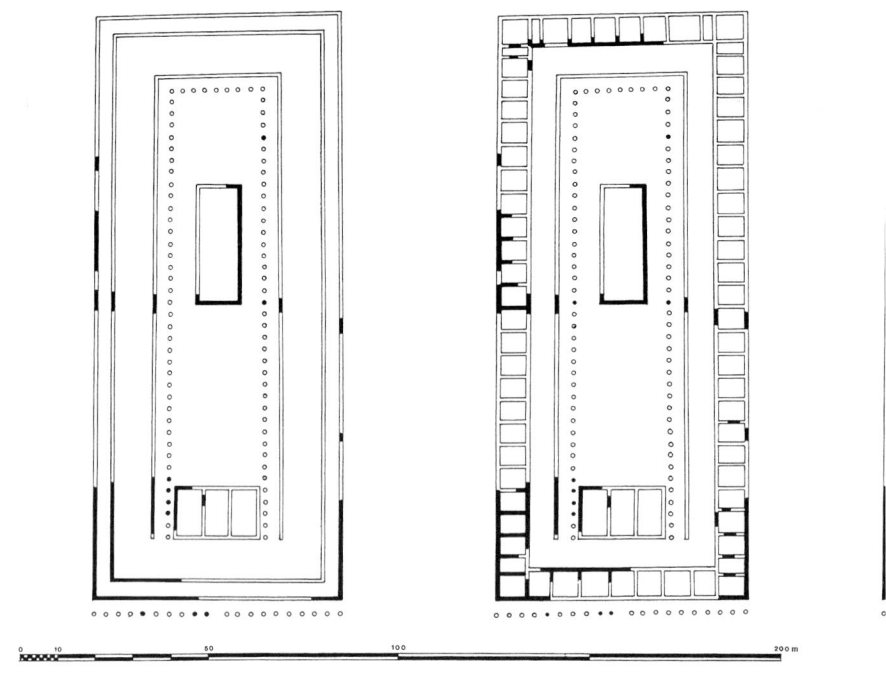

DM '99

Ill IV.8 Courtyard building behind headquarters as originally designed.
(*left*) and as completed (*right*): plans (Scale 1/2000)

least, and it is evident that the structures in this area are in some way bound up with the reason for the fortress's unusually large size. Immediately behind the *principia* lay a building of courtyard plan (Ill IV.8). Its south-west corner was excavated in 1967/8, but it was only with excavations further north in 1979–81 that the enormous size of this building became apparent when it was revealed to measure 60 m in width and 160 m in length and occupied the space equivalent to two full *insulae*. It consisted of a narrow outer range which was separated from an inner free-standing colonnaded portico by an open space. At the heart of the complex was a single, long rectangular structure some 12 by 30 m in size. Another unusual feature was the fact that it was built of stone, not timber. Construction had only got as far as ground level when work stopped, and there was an interval possibly lasting a decade or more before the building was completed, albeit to a modified plan in which the outer range was widened from 6 to 8.5 m and divided up into rooms of regular size with wide doorways. As completed, the building appears to have been used for storage purposes.

To the west of the south end of the building just described lay the so-called Elliptical Building, a structure which has been the subject of intense speculation ever since the final campaign of excavation in the late 1960s (Ill IV.9). It has been a source of puzzlement because no building even remotely like it has been found in any other legionary fortress anywhere in the empire. Attempts to define its function were hampered for many years by the failure of the director of the 1960s excavations to produce a detailed plan, let alone a

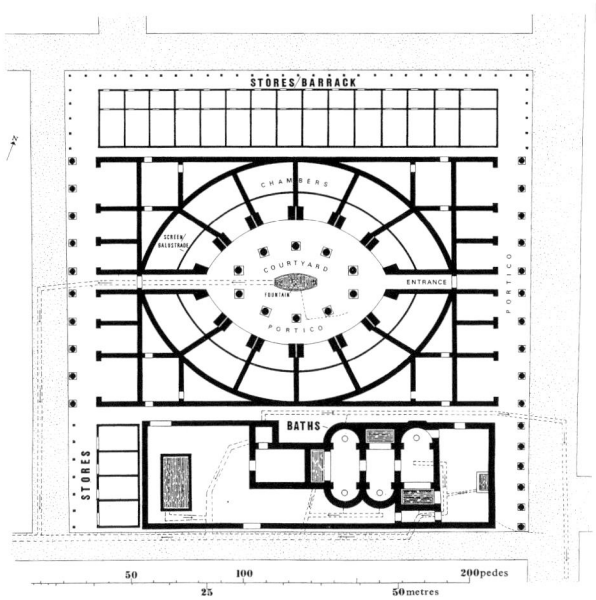

Ill IV.9 Flavian Elliptical Building and neighbouring structures: restored and corrected plan.
(Scale 1/1000). (Copyright D Mason and Chester City Council)

definitive report. This omission has now been remedied by the recent publication of a comprehensive account of this building. The Elliptical Building measured 60 x 33 m overall and consisted of a central oval courtyard 9 x 14 m in size surrounded by a 4-m-deep colonnaded portico behind which lay an encircling range of twelve wedge-shaped rooms. All of the latter were equipped with monumental-scale arched entrances 4 m wide and at least 5.5 m high which were raised on stone piers 1.8 x 0.90 m in size arranged in pairs and set on very hard cobble concrete foundations 2.5 m square and 1 m thick formed in rock-cut pits. A short way into the interior lay a slight foundation concentric with the other elements which can have supported little more than a screen or balustrade. At the heart of the courtyard lay the foundation for some form of monument which we know was to include a fountain as a lead water pipe was found running up to its base. This bore a moulded inscription recording its manufacture during the ninth consulship of Vespasian and the seventh of his son Titus (AD 79, before 24 June) when Gnaeus Julius Agricola was governor of Britain (Ill IV.10). Cut into the rock floor of the foundation pit along one side was a small trench which had been filled with clean earth (Ill IV.11). This seems likely to have been connected with some form of foundation ceremony at the time of the building's inception.

To reconcile it with the surrounding street grid, the main part of the building was enclosed within a rectilinear perimeter wall, and a range of rooms along the shorter sides completed the plan. Access to the interior of the building was limited to a narrow entrance at each end of the long axis. The northern end of the *insula* was occupied by long narrow store building, while most of the southern end was taken up by a bath building. Much smaller than

III IV.10 Lead water pipe serving fountain at centre of Elliptical Building courtyard; the cast inscription mentions the number of consulships held by Vespasian and his son Titus, enabling the pipe's manufacture to be placed in the first half of the year 79.
(Copyright D Mason and Chester City Council)

III IV.11 Foundation for fountain at centre of Elliptical Building courtyard, as revealed by mechanical excavation in 1964. Note the ritual trench cut into the rock floor of the foundation pit along the left side. (Copyright D Mason and Chester City Council)

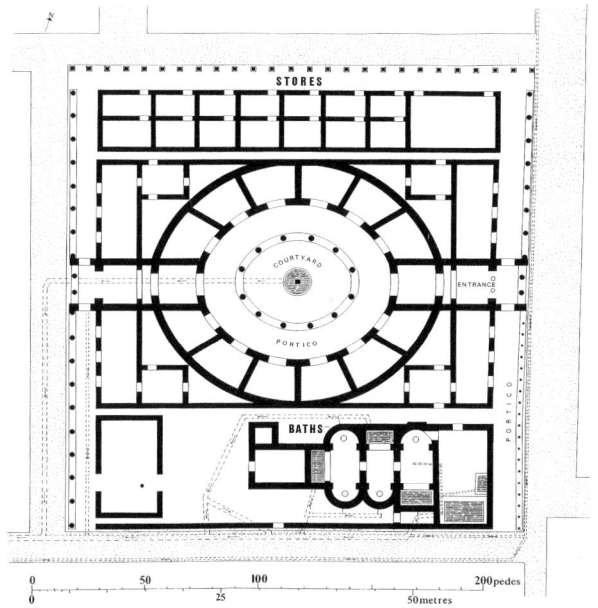

III IV.12 Second Elliptical Building, erected *c* AD 230, and neighbouring structures: restored plan. (Scale 1/1000). (Copyright D Mason and Chester City Council)

the fortress baths, these are an additional oddity as legionary fortresses normally have only one internal bath building.

Like the enormous building to the east, construction of the Elliptical Building stopped soon after the foundations and footings had been laid. Here, however, the subsequent interval before completion was far longer — 150 years in fact. The site lay largely derelict, used for the dumping of refuse which buried the wall stubs of the building beneath a layer 1 m thick. The project was resurrected when the fortress underwent a comprehensive rebuilding in the period *c* 230 and this time the Elliptical Building was actually finished, though with major modifications to the original design (Ill IV.12). These included less monumental entrances to the twelve principal rooms and the deletion of the screen wall, a complete physical separation of the oval and street-frontage ranges, a tripling in the size of the two entrances to the building, which also received far grander architectural treatment, and the possible addition of a second storey. It is quite evident from the relationship between the foundations of the original and later buildings that the location of the former was completely unknown to the surveyors who laid out the third-century building. This means that they must have had access to the 150-year-old plans of the original structure which had presumably lain in the fortress archives gathering dust for a century and a half — an interesting insight into Roman military record-keeping.

Because of its uniqueness, and the absence of internal fittings and commemorative inscriptions owing to its unfinished state, the intended function of the original Elliptical Building is problematical. The quality of its construction shows that it was an extremely important structure, but beyond that one can only study its architectural form to see how it could actually function as a building in order to try and determine its purpose. It was certainly not suitable as a residence, nor was it linked with the neighbouring baths in such a way as to suggest they were parts of a single complex. Similarly, neither the layout of the substructure nor the size and shape of the courtyard support the notion that it was some form of amphitheatre. It does bear a superficial resemblance to a number of market buildings, but it is difficult to see why such a mundane structure would have been given this elaborate architectural treatment, and in any case a market is not the sort of building to be found inside a military base, at least not at this period.

The overall design was clearly intended to achieve an enclosed and quiet atmosphere, while the twelve equal-sized rooms with their open, monumental doorways seem built specifically for the purpose of display. The fact that there are twelve chambers may be important as this number, then as now, possessed multi-facetted significance, not least in both terrestrial and cosmological mapping. The twelve months of the year and the twelve major points on the compass spring to mind, as do the twelve principal deities of the Roman state. The last of these would have been a suitable subject for the contents of the rooms, but there is in fact no evidence from elsewhere of the 'divine dozen' being worshipped in a single building. Also, apart from the shrine containing a likeness of the emperor in the headquarters building, temples and shrines were confined to the area outside the defences. The number twelve does, however, occur in the context of the division of the empire into administrative units, and so does its multiple twenty-four in the early first-century descriptive account which accompanied Agrippa's pictorial map of the empire set up in Rome *c* 5 BC. Then there is the very unusual and awkward shape of the main part of the building, which must be significant as the architect had taken so much trouble to achieve this rather than a simpler design. It is surely no mere coincidence that it is very reminiscent of the shape of the inhabited world — the *orbis terrarum* — as perceived by Roman and earlier geographers. Thus, the Elliptical Building could have been an 'image of the world' or *imago mundi*, the fountain and accompanying pool at its centre representing the Mediterranean, with the surrounding rooms containing sculpture, statuary, frescoes and/or mosaics depicting the countries and peoples of the constituent regions of the empire, presided over by the all powerful, semi-divine emperor ensuring Rome did not falter from its ordained destiny to rule the world.

If this were its true purpose, why was such an unusual and extravagant building, more in keeping with the architecture of a major city, or even Rome itself, constructed in a straightforwardly utilitarian establishment like a legionary fortress, especially one at the very edge of the empire? It might be explained by the close link between the legion which founded Chester, II *Adiutrix pia fidelis*, and the emperor Vespasian. The final contest in the period of civil war which became known as the 'year of the four emperors' (68/9) was between the forces of Vitellius and those of Vespasian. At a critical moment in the battle for the control of Italy, the section of the Mediterranean fleet based at Ravenna went over to Vespasian's side, and as a reward the men involved were enrolled in a new legion — II *Adiutrix* — with the higher status and greater privileges this bestowed. Soon afterwards the legion was dispatched to Lower Germany to assist in the suppression of the revolt of Civilis, and thence to Britain in 71, where it took over the fortress at Lincoln from Legion

Ill IV.13 Massive masonry and elaborate cornice of fortress curtain wall

IX which moved forward to York. Chester was the first fortress that II *Adiutrix* actually built for itself, and this might explain the inclusion of a building which celebrated Vespasian both as Restorer of Peace to the Roman world (just like the first emperor Augustus, to whom he was often compared) and founder of a new dynasty — the Flavians.

While this might explain the Elliptical Building, it does not account for the other peculiarities of the Chester fortress. The curtain wall of the defences, for example, is unusually grand in that it is built of very large blocks of sandstone laid without mortar in the style known as *opus quadratum* (Ill IV.13). Requiring much greater skill to construct than the more common double-skinned concrete walls with *petit appareil* facings found at York and Caerleon, this style was already rather archaic by the mid-first century, being reserved for particularly important structures such as city gates, temple podia and the walls of those most Roman of provincial cities — colonies of legionary veterans. The date of the completion of the fortress wall at Chester is unknown but, as described above, there is sound evidence that it was begun in the early Flavian period.

There are also the baths next to the Elliptical Building and the large building behind the *principia* already mentioned, while the early disruption of the construction programme exhibited by both of these also affected the *insula* north of the Elliptical Building. There, whatever structure was intended for the bulk of the plot was not even begun let alone finished, and it remained open ground until the third century. Clearly, there had been some grand scheme planned for the centre of the fortress, consisting of at least three unusual buildings, which had been abandoned at an early stage in its development. That these were not essential to the normal functioning of the fortress is shown by the fact that the sites of two of them remained largely unused for 150 years, while another was completed but to a modified plan. It is obvious that it was the 'extra' buildings at the heart of the fortress that caused it to be 20% larger than its sister fortresses, and if the three *insulae* just described are grouped together in a symmetrical arrangement with the two on the east side of the large building and the peculiarly shallow plots to the north they total *c* 4 ha, the amount by which Chester exceeds the size of Caerleon and York (Ill IV.14). It is equally obvious that these buildings were rather special and that the extra space was not required merely to accommodate additional barracks or stores. Taken together with the unusual form and architectural sophistication of the Elliptical Building it seems very likely that it was an authority higher even than the legate of the legion that ordered the construction of these extra buildings, in other words it was a decision taken by the provincial governor himself, who intended to make Chester his headquarters and thus the *de facto* administrative centre for the entire province. Thus, the lead water mains at Chester bearing the name of the provincial governor, which are the only examples from the whole of Britain, should perhaps be taken at face value as evidence of buildings under his direct control.

This suggestion might seem outlandish, but Chester had a lot to recommend it as the location for the governor's headquarters in this period. The collapse of the client-kingdom of Brigantia and its annexation by Rome in the early 70s, together with the final subjugation of the Ordovices in north-west Wales, had more than doubled the size of the province. The expansionist policy adopted by the Flavians in Britain, where both Vespasian and Titus had seen action, the former commanding Legion II *Augusta* during the invasion period, required a base for the governor which was closer to the centre of the action than Colchester, the existing headquarters. Chester lay equidistant from the other legionary bases at Caerleon and York, with its rear protected by Wroxeter, had good communications back to the south-east and, very importantly, possessed an excellent harbour well suited to be the base for combined land and sea operations along the west coast. It also faced out towards Ireland which we know Agricola, and possibly his predecessor Sextus Frontinus, had already targeted for future conquest. And what more appropriate place for the representative of the semi-divine being of the emperor to exercise power from than *Deva*, whose very name carried connotations of powerful divinity in both Latin and Celtic?

An additional 4 ha might seem an excessive amount of space merely to cater for the governor, but it must be remembered that he was accompanied by his personal retinue of friends and advisers, a bodyguard of 1,000 troops and a considerable body of officials and administrators. These would have needed offices as well as living accommodation, while an audience hall where the governor could receive and hold meetings with representatives of the British tribes would have been a necessity. Possibly the vast building behind the *principia* was intended to be the principal administrative complex, with the governor's residence occupying one of the plots on its east side. As to the Elliptical Building, the inclusion in the government compound of a monument which celebrated the majesty of Rome and its restored sense of purpose under the founder of a new dynasty would have been especially appropriate given that both the legion in residence — II *Adiutrix* — and the men who held the office or governor during its construction — Sextus Julius Frontinus (74–7) and Gnaeus Julius Agricola (77–83) — had strong ties with the emperor Vespasian. Who among the British delegates visiting

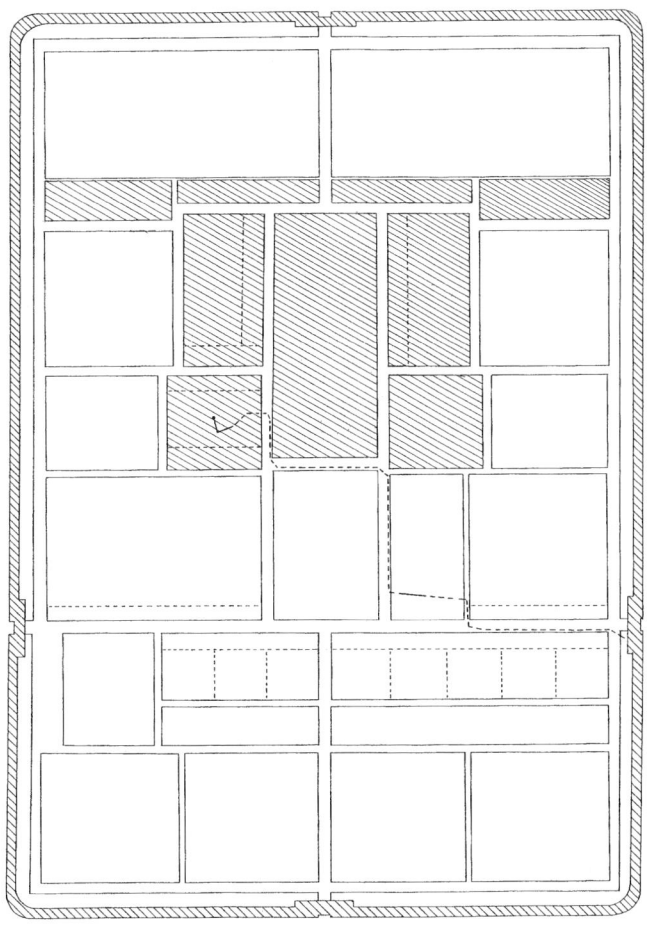

III IV.14 Area of fortress reserved for offices and accommodation of the provincial governor
and his staff: block plan. (Scale 1/5000).
(Copyright D Mason and Chester City Council)

Deva would not have been impressed either by the extent and power of Rome as depicted by its contents or by the creature comforts available in the baths next door? Nor were the military successes in Britain used for purely local propaganda purposes. Back in Rome, Vespasian and Titus in 75 presided over the ceremonial extending of the city's formal limits (something which had happened on only two previous occasions: Caesar's conquest of Gaul and Claudius' invasion of Britain), symbolising the extension of the empire based on their conquests in that distant island.

If this indeed was the grand plan for Chester, what caused it to be abandoned? The answer is very probably bound up with the decision to conquer the tribes beyond the Brigantes. Agricola's campaigns in Scotland shifted the focus of activity much farther north. Combined operations by the legions and the fleet featured prominently and II *Adiutrix* may have been heavily involved, given its maritime background, and this may have caused the construction programme at Chester to be postponed. It is also possible that Frontinus' choice of Chester as headquarters no longer suited Agricola. No sooner had Scotland been conquered than it was rapidly abandoned because of Domitian's need to withdraw troops to repel Dacian incursions across the Danube. Thoughts of further conquest in Britain were given up: by the close of the first century the governors of Britain were more likely to be administrators than generals, and London, the commercial hub of the province, had become the obvious location for the seat of the administration.

Amongst the range of decorated antefixes found at Chester there are two types which stand out from the rest, not only because they are comparatively rare and the emblems they bear are different from the ubiquitous boar of Legion XX but also, and principally, because the quality of the moulds from which they were cast is exceptionally fine. One shows a lion's head and the other the face of Jupiter in his guise as the horned god Jupiter Ammon (Ill IV.15). That is the only difference, however, and their shared high quality and common overall design — with the central image framed in an *aedicula* with spirally fluted columns — demonstrates that the two types were contemporary. At what period they were in use is unknown, although I feel their exquisite quality is indicative of an early date. Most examples have been recovered as stray finds, while those found during excavation have occurred as single items in refuse deposits. However, it may be significant that there are no examples in the large collection of antefixes recovered from the site of Legion XX's brick, tile and pottery works at Holt, 12 km south of Chester, which were in use from *c* AD 90 to *c* AD 240. They are far too fine to be of local civilian manufacture and the possibility must be considered, therefore, that they were made by Legion II Adiutrix. While this cannot be proved the iconography of these antefixes supports that notion.

Amun (also Amen, Amon, Ammon) was the chief of the Egyptian gods. One of the sacred animals associated with Amun was the ram and he was often depicted with a ram's head. His popularity also spread to the tribes of the Libyan desert and one of his centres of worship was the oasis at Siwa. The fame of the oracle at the latter spread throughout the eastern Mediterranean with the growth of major Greek colonies in Egypt from the eighth century BC; and when Alexander the Great put an end to Persian rule in Egypt in the 330s it was the oasis at Siwa that he made a point of visiting, despite the hazardous journey involved. The oracle (of course) pronounced him 'Son of Ammon' and thus the rightful

III IV.15 Examples of two types of antefix possibly associated with Legion II *Adiutrix*.
One bears the bearded and horned head of Jupiter Ammon, the other the head
of a lion — the zodiacal sign associated with Jupiter.
(Copyright Chester City Council, Grosvenor Museum)

ruler of Egypt. The unifier of Greece and Asia, Alexander was referred to by Persian poets in later years as 'Sikandar Dhulkharnein' — meaning 'Alexander the Two-horned' — because he and his successor Hellenistic rulers were often portrayed on coinage with the horns of Amun, a device meant to convey their divine right to rule. The usual process of syncretism led to Zeus Ammon becoming the chief god of the Hellenistic world represented by an image of the head of Zeus replete with the horns of Amun.

In 30 BC, Octavian (shortly to become the emperor Augustus) became sole ruler of the entire Graeco-Roman world, including Egypt, and for the first time since Alexander all of the hellenised countries of the east were united. A master of propaganda, Augustus used the image of Jupiter Ammon (Zeus having been supplanted by Jupiter with Rome's mastery of Greece) to promote the image of the universal extent and semi-divine nature of his power. In the Forum of Augustus in Rome, for example, the attic storey of the portico surrounding the Temple of Mars Ultor was embellished with decorated roundels containing portraits of Jupiter Ammon and Medusa, a scheme alluding to his decisive defeat of Mark Antony's forces at Actium and subsequent conquest of Egypt by evoking memories of Alexander's hanging of gold shields on the Parthenon in 334 BC in celebration of his victory over Darius. Imitations of this decorative scheme soon appeared in the *fora* and imperial cult sanctuaries at major provincial centres in the west including Arles, Avenches, Geneva, Merida, Tarragona, and Vienne. More pertinent to the present discussion, it was also deployed in the civic buildings of ports in the northern Adriatic such as Aquileia, Concordia, Trieste and Zara, the very region where the section of the fleet from which Legion II *Adiutrix* was raised had its base. The site of early Roman Ravenna has been little explored and so the employment there of the Jupiter Ammon image in architectural decoration cannot be proved. Even so, it would have been very familiar to the men who were enrolled in II *Adiutrix*.

Furthermore, their allegiance to Vespasian in the civil war of 69, for which they were rewarded with legionary status and the title *pia fidelis*, 'loyal and faithful', may have given them a particular reason to promote this emblem. Although Vespasian was the eventual victor of the civil war of 68/9, he was the founder of a new dynasty and the first Italian (as opposed to Roman) emperor, and as such he needed to generate as much propaganda as possible to demonstrate the legitimacy of his rule to try and deter any further rivals. The similarities with Augustus were heavily promoted, especially the role of 'restorer of peace and saviour of the empire'. Even older parallels were invoked. Vespasian was first acclaimed emperor at Alexandria and like that city's founder, whom Augustus too had been so keen to imitate, was saluted as 'son of Ammon' as well as 'Caesar the god'. The acclamations were led by the prefect of Egypt whose name, ironically, was Tiberius Julius Alexander. Vespasian and his supporters thus had good reasons for adopting and promoting the Jupiter Ammon image with its connotations of universal power and divine protection and this, I believe, explains its occurrence at Flavian Chester. But why, you ask, was the lion's head used as an accompanying emblem? It is true that the lion was particularly associated with Hercules and was thus symbolic of great physical strength, an admirable quality for a legion. However, perhaps even more telling, the lion was also the zodiacal sign of Jupiter.

Further reading

Brushfield, T N 1885	The Roman remains of Chester with a particular description of those discovered in Bridge Street in 1863. *J Chester Archaeol Soc* old ser **3**, 1–106
Carrington, P 1985	The Roman advance into the north-west Midlands before AD 71. *J Chester Archaeol Soc* new ser **68**, 5–22
Dilke, O A W 1985	Greek and Roman maps. London: Thames & Hudson
Levick, B 1999	Vespasian. London: Routledge
McPeake, J C 1978	The first century AD. In: Strickland, T J & Davey, P J eds. New evidence for Roman Chester. Liverpool University, 9–16
Mason, D J P 2000	Excavations at Chester, The Elliptical Building: an image of the Roman world? Excavations in 1939 and 1963–9. Chester City Council. (Chester Archaeol Excav Surv Rep **12**)
Mason, D J P *forthcoming*	Excavations at Chester, the baths of the legionary fortress: investigations 1732–1988. Chester City Council. (Chester Archaeol Excav Surv Rep **13**)
Nicolet, C 1991	Space, geography and politics in the early Roman empire. Ann Arbor: Univ Michigan
Petch, D F 1968	The *praetorium* at Deva. *J Chester Archaeol Soc* new ser **55**, 1–5
Petch, D F 1971	Excavations on the site of the Old Market Hall, Chester: a second summary report. *J Chester Archaeol Soc* new ser **57**, 3–26

Small, A ed 1996   Subject and ruler: the cult of the ruling power in classical antiquity. Ann Arbor: Univ Michigan (*J Roman Archaeol* supp ser **17**)

Strickland, T J 1982   Chester: excavations in the Princess Street/Hunter Street area, 1978–82. A first report on discoveries of the Roman period. *J Chester Archaeol Soc* new ser **65**, 5–24

V: The Town and Port of Roman Chester

by D J P Mason PhD, FSA, MIFA

The Town

veterani et cives Romani et consistentes ad canabas legionis XX valeriae victricis

As well as being an important military base Deva was also a significant civilian centre and a major port. Like any military unit, the legion installed at Chester was accompanied by a considerable number of civilian 'hangers on'. Once thought by modern writers to be simply camp followers whose presence was barely tolerated by the military authorities, research in recent years has shown that certain classes of civilians were not merely allowed to settle beside camps and forts but, because of their close links with the army, were positively encouraged to do so, with land and facilities being set aside for their use. Many such civilians were engaged in commerce, such as sutlers (*lixae*), traders (*negotiatores*) and merchants (*mercatores*) who made their living by supplying the soldiers with a wide range of commodities and luxuries. On occasion, such men also supplied army units with specific goods in volume on a contractual basis. There were also those who set up establishments which provided the diversions and entertainments of greatest appeal to the ordinary soldier in his off-duty hours, namely taverns, brothels and gambling dens. Another group which comprised a sizeable proportion of the civilian community consisted of the common-law wives of troops (until the reforms of the early third century serving soldiers could not contract legal marriages) and their children. Also, every year about 300 men of Legion XX reached the end of their term of service. Although some would have moved away from Chester, either to settle in another part of Britain (the hinterland of Wroxeter or perhaps the prosperous south-east) or even to return to their ancestral homelands abroad, others set up home in the extramural settlement beside the fortress (*canabae legionis*), legitimised their previously informal unions and raised their sons as future recruits for the legion.

Already quite substantial within a few years, settlements of this type soon grew to a town-like size, and inscriptions from *canabae* elsewhere show that they possessed their own council and appointed officials, copying those in formally constituted towns and cities, to see to the running of their everyday affairs. Inscriptions from a number of sites record public actions or communal dedications made by such communities, in which the various constituent elements of the population are mentioned thus: *veterani et cives Romani et consistentes ad canabas legionis*, meaning 'veterans and Roman citizens and others gathered together at the *canabae* of the legion ...'.

The existence of suburbs around the Chester fortress has long been known, but it is only in comparatively recent years that their extent, character and history have begun to be clarified to any degree (Ill V.1). To the east of the fortress, evidence which has accumulated in a piecemeal fashion over many years points to intensive development fronting both sides of the main road (perpetuated by modern Foregate Street) and consisting for the most part of small rectangular buildings positioned end-on to the road. These conform to the well-known 'strip building' category of Roman structures which predominated in the commercial quarters of Roman towns and cities and which consisted of a shop at the front, a store or workshop behind and residential apartments at the rear and/or above. The earliest buildings, as one might expect, were timber and were replaced in the early years of the second century by more substantial structures partly or wholly constructed of stone. Although the evidence indicates street-frontage development stretching out from the fortress east gate for some considerable distance, the discovery of extensive rubbish dumps in the City Road/Dee Lane area suggests that the built-up area did not extend any further than about 300 m.

To the north of the road, immediately outside the east gate, lay the legionary parade ground or *campus*, partially explored in 1966. While the general impression of the remainder of the backland areas behind the street frontage is one of open ground used for industrial activities, possibly including the manufacture of pottery and glass as well as metal-working, excavation of a site in Priory Place in 1989 by Simon Ward demonstrated that side streets with their own intensive street-frontage development also existed, at least in the southern half of this area. This side street lay about 200 m out from the fortress defences and two stone strip buildings, each approximately 8 m wide and 25 m long, were found fronting its east side about 110 m south of Foregate Street. Erected around AD 120, they would seem to represent expansion into the backland zone. Traces of at least two other side streets have been found closer in to the fortress, although evidence of accompanying buildings was less conclusive.

Early excavations and observations noted sections of ditches of differing size and profile at various points in the eastern suburbs, but their purpose remains obscure. One such, following an east-west alignment to the south of Foregate Street, was apparently already obsolete by the close of the first century and may have belonged to a construction camp associated with the building of the fortress. At least one other was of much later date and may conceivably have belonged to a system of defences erected around the eastern *canabae* in the later Roman period.

Moving round to the area south of the fortress, the land opposite the south-east angle was occupied largely by the military amphitheatre (*ludus*). Discovered in 1929, its northern half was excavated in the 1960s, followed by consolidation works to enable its remains to be displayed (Ill V.2). The earliest *ludus*, built soon after the foundation of the fortress, was of timber and measured 67 x *c* 75 m overall. This was soon replaced by a much larger stone structure measuring 87.2 x *c* 95.7 m, which had a seating capacity more than twice that of its predecessor. Since purchasing Dee House, which overlies the other half of the amphitheatre, in the mid-1990s Chester City Council has been exploring ways of achieving the exposure of further portions of this impressive structure, the largest known military

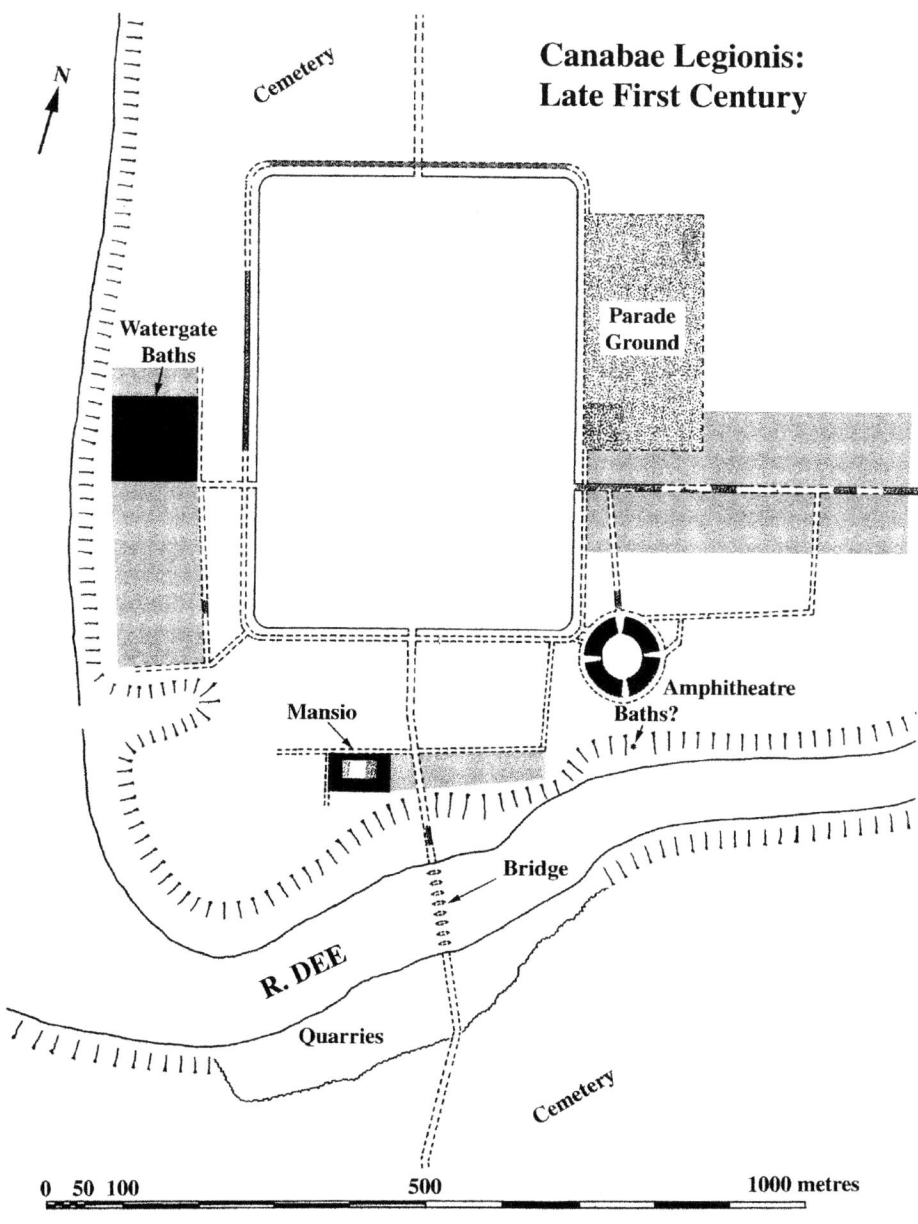

III V.1 Extent of *canabae legionis c* AD 100: plan. (Scale 1/10 000). Solid black = known buildings; shading = general extent of built-up area)

amphitheatre in Britain. Mechanical sounding of a site south of the amphitheatre in 1989 encountered a substantial structure of brick and concrete set on a terrace beside the Dee, an ideal spot for the location of a bath building serving visitors to the amphitheatre.

The area south of the fortress was bisected by the road (now Lower Bridge Street) which ran down to the bridge across the Dee. To either side of this road, a zone stretching 150 m out from the defences appears to have been kept deliberately free of any major structures, although some evidence for industrial activity has been recovered. Further south, however, beyond the line of present-day Castle Street and Duke Street, evidence recovered during the last twenty years proves the existence of a number of substantial, well appointed buildings occupying prime sites along the edge of the sandstone plateau overlooking the river. The discovery in the nineteenth century of a finely constructed wall at the eastern extremity of the area beside the City Walls has been supplemented in the 1990s by the exposure in evaluation trenches south of Duke Street of other elements of solid masonry structures further west, including one with an apsidal room. West of Lower Bridge Street, excavations in 1976 exposed part of a large courtyard building with a long and com-

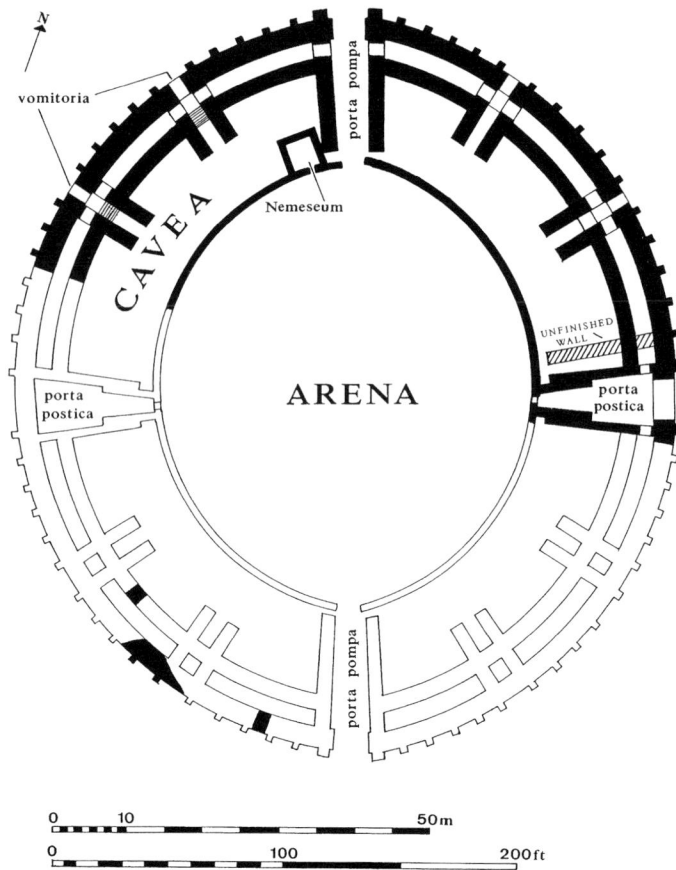

III V.2 Stone legionary amphitheatre *c* AD 100: plan. (Scale 1/1000)

III V.3 *Mansio c* AD 180: plan. (Scale 1/1250). (Copyright Chester City Council)

plicated history. Tentatively identified as a *mansio* — lodgings principally for government employees travelling on official business — the earliest phase of this building, in timber, was erected shortly after the establishment of the fortress and for a time was linked directly with the south gate of the latter by a dedicated trackway.

The initial *mansio* was destroyed by fire. Two further phases of timber building followed, both of which extended farther to the east than the original. The last of these was demolished *c* AD 120, and work began on the construction of a stone replacement laid out to a new design. This was soon abandoned, however, and after an interval a new stone *mansio* was erected with a plan similar to its timber predecessors. This included a colonnaded portico along its southern frontage which took advantage of the magnificent view over the Dee below (Ill V.3). A well was provided under the cover of this portico and a second was added at the end of the second century when further building works were carried out (Ill V.4). The refurbished building continued in use down to the end of the third century, when much of the *mansio* was destroyed by a catastrophic fire. This had claimed the lives of at least two of the occupants whose remains were cast along with other debris into one of the wells as part of the subsequent clearing-up operation. New structures were then erected and remained in use until the middle of the fourth century. A notable item found re-used in their foundations was an altar dedicated to the *numina* or 'guiding spirits'

Ill V.4 Head of well under portico on south side of *mansio*. (Copyright Chester City Council)

of the emperors by a person whose name began Com[.... , one of the few inscriptions found in Chester in recent years (Ill V.5).

The *mansio* would have had its own bath building, and antiquarian accounts of discoveries in the area suggest that this may have lain to the east, beside the road leading down to the bridge. Exploration of the area lying west and south-west of the *mansio* has been impeded by the medieval and later buildings of Chester Castle, although structural remains encountered during its early nineteenth-century remodelling suggest the existence of at least one substantial Roman building in this area. Downhill from the *mansio* fragments of a succession of Roman buildings were found close to the west side of the bridgehead in 1983, while excavations in Edgar's Field in Handbridge in 1996 demonstrated that the built-up area extended to the opposite bank of the River Dee, where lay the principal legionary quarries.

It is, however, in the western sector of the *canabae* that the greatest amount of new information has been recovered over the last twenty-five years. This area formed a quite distinct and well defined part of the extramural settlement, consisting of the 180-m-wide strip of land lying between the fortress and the harbour and separated from the southern sector by a large natural declivity which extended from the Roodee almost as far as the south-west angle of the fortress. Earlier chance discoveries had hinted at the presence of buildings of some quality in this area, while an excavation at the south-west corner of Lower Watergate Street, which roughly perpetuates the line of a road running from the fortress west gate to the harbour, had shown that considerable landscaping and terracing operations had been undertaken to accommodate them. Excavations carried out between 1974 and 1988 on a number of sites further south — principally Greyfriars Court,

Ill V.5 Altar found in *mansio* dedicated *numinbus Augustorum*, ie 'to the guiding spirits of the Emperors'. (Copyright Chester City Council)

Greyfriars House and Nicholas Street Mews — revealed the area to be densely packed with buildings, many of which were of good-quality masonry construction in their second-century and later manifestations, equipped with concrete floors, hypocausts and, in the case of that occupying the south-west corner of the area, its own private baths suite (Ill V.6). Most if not all of these buildings were apparently residential, and it would appear that this area was the 'up market' sector of the *canabae*. The development of this area had commenced early on, and late first-century timber buildings, at least one of which may have been an official store, were found beneath the later structures on the Greyfriars Court site.

Further north, remains found during the construction of town houses at the bottom end of Lower Watergate Street in 1778/9, together with chance discoveries made during later building operations in areas nearby, suggested the presence of a very large and imposing building. These discoveries included very thick walls and hypocausts as well as mosaic floors, implying it could have been the main extramural bath building. The first opportunity to test this theory in modern times came in 1989 with the building of an extension to Sedan House, which lies at the corner of City Walls Road and Stanley Place. Excavation

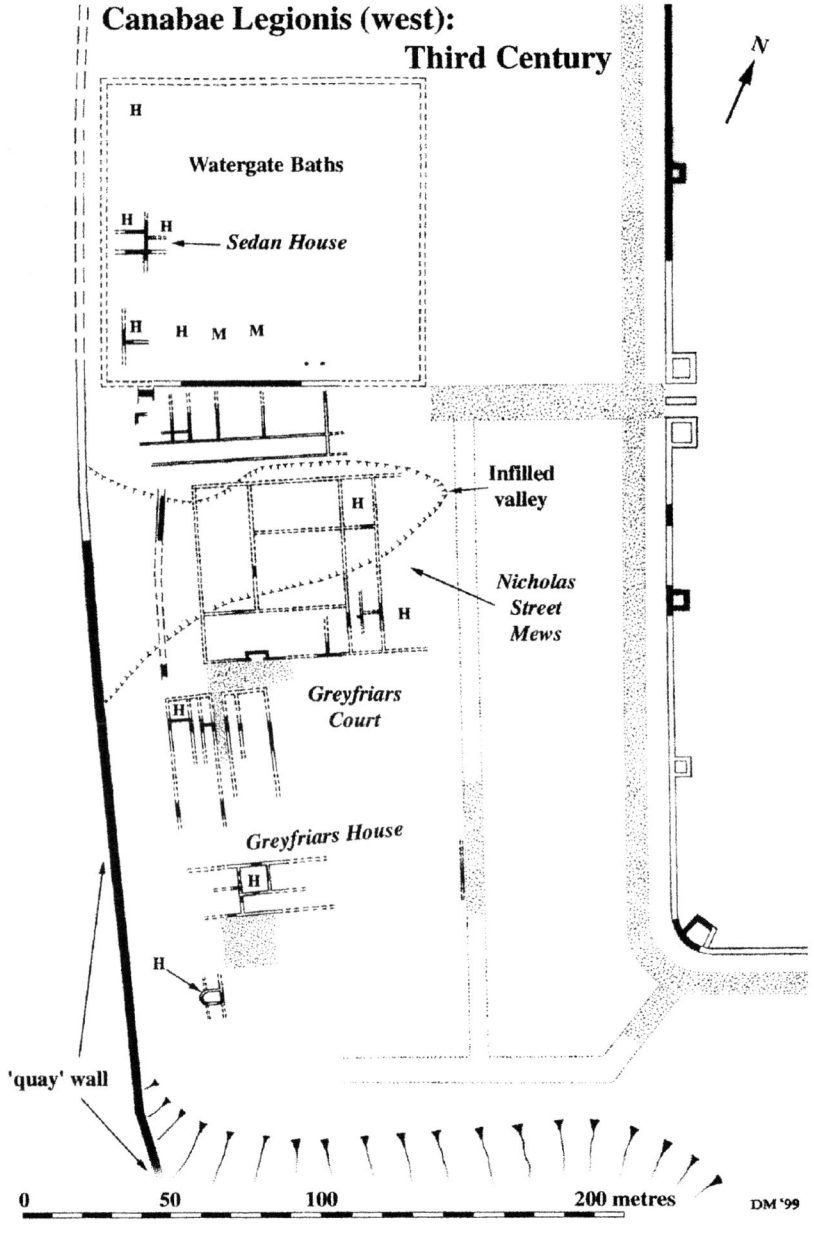

Canabae Legionis (west):
Third Century

N

H

Watergate Baths

H H ←— *Sedan House*

H H M M

Infilled valley

Nicholas Street Mews

H

Greyfriars Court

H

Greyfriars House

H

H

'quay' wall

0   50   100   200 metres   DM '99

III V.6 Western sector of the *canabae c* AD 200: plan. (Scale 1/2500)

Ill V.7 Baths in Lower Watergate Street: Sedan House excavation 1989, showing remains of latest flooring. (Copyright Chester City Council)

exposed parts of several rooms in this complex, all with a very complicated structural history, while the quality and substantial nature of the masonry and the presence of both concrete and herringbone-pattern tiled floors, hypocausts, a plunge bath and complex drainage systems confirmed that it was indeed an important bath building (Ill V.7). Taken together with the other structural remains of a similar character found in the vicinity, this bath building appears to have covered an area approximately 100 m square, that is about one third greater than the main fortress baths. It is almost certainly the presence of the substantial remains of this building which explains the westward deviation in the course of the City Walls at this point.

Undoubtedly built by the legion, the constructional characteristics of some of the earliest features of this building would suggest it was erected not long after the foundation of the fortress. The early provision of a large extramural bathing complex, supplementary to the intramural baths, is a feature found at many fortresses and indicates official recognition of the attendant civilian community as being indivisible from the legion and approval of the construction of facilities especially for their use. No doubt the military authorities saw the worth of promoting high standards of hygiene and cleanliness among those with whom the soldiers frequently consorted.

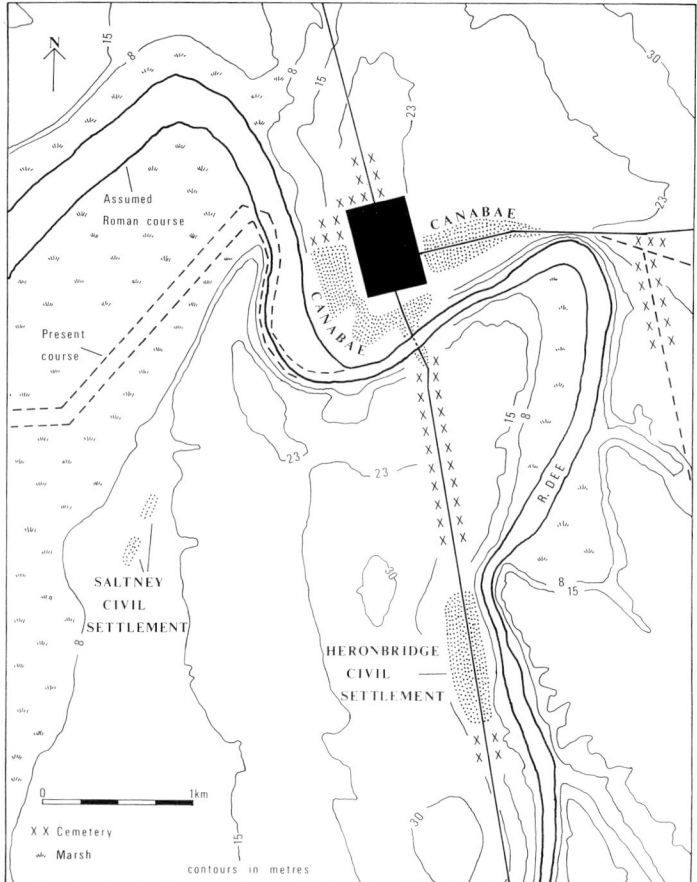

III V.8 Location of Heronbridge and Saltney settlements: plan.
(Scale 1/50 000)

There is sufficient evidence to prove that buildings continued for some distance north of the baths, but exploration has been very limited and their date and purpose remain unknown. Much of the northern portion of this area, however, remained as open ground throughout the Roman period and was used as an inhumation cemetery in the mid- to late second century.

Evidence for civilian settlement along the road heading north from the fortress towards the Wirral is still lacking despite many years of observation and recording, and it seems probable that this area was used largely, if not exclusively, as a burial ground. Cemeteries also lined the other roads heading out from the fortress beyond the built-up areas. Possibly the largest of these lay on the opposite side of the river, encompassing the land beyond the quarries and lining the road which ran south to Whitchurch for a distance of about 1 km. Burials have also been found at the outer edge of the land south-west of the fortress, while another group, apparently all cremations and thus probably comparatively early, lay

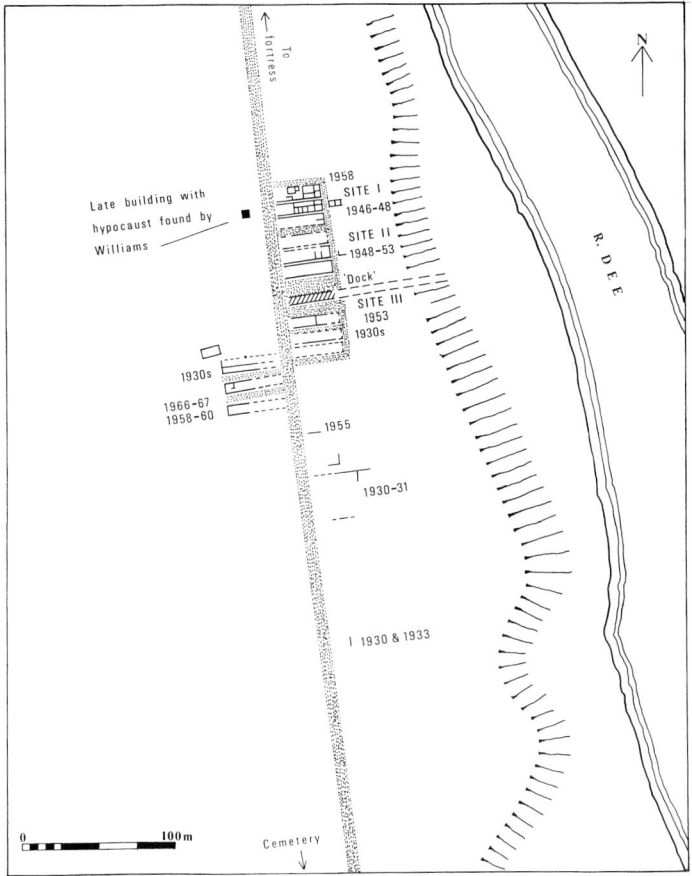

III V.9 Heronbridge: plan showing layout of stone strip buildings *c* AD 130.
(Scale 1/5000)

clustered in the vicinity of the source of the legionary aqueduct at Boughton 1.5 km east of the fortress.

The suburbs immediately beside the fortress did not, however, constitute the totality of civilian settlement at Chester. As at the majority of legionary fortresses there was another civilian community of urban-like form only a few kilometres away, in Chester's case at Heronbridge astride the road running sooth to Whitchurch (Ill V.8). The last major campaign of excavation here in the l960s demonstrated that occupation had begun *c* AD 90 and continued down to at least the middle of the third century. As in the eastern sector of the *canabae*, the majority of buildings were strip houses set end-on to the main road (Ill V.9). Retailing was clearly an important part of its economy, and evidence for both the production of bronze objects and the processing of grain was recovered. The reasons for the phenomenon of settlement duality at legionary bases are unknown but it is thought to be bound up with differences between the constitutional and territorial status of the two communities. That lying next to the fortress stood on ground owned by the legion (the *territorium* or *prata legionis*), where civilians could only be tenants, whereas that further out lay outside its boundary on the territory of the neighbouring *civitas* and thus had greater autonomy, with its inhabitants being able to own the land where they lived.

To complete the picture of civilian settlement there was another community at Saltney, 2 km south-west of the fortress. Hastily excavated in the 1920s, this appears to have been a much poorer community consisting of single, crudely constructed dwellings set in fenced and ditched enclosures. Agriculture may have been the basis of its economy.

Finally, the existence of a cremation cemetery (and thus presumably of second-century date or earlier) 1.5 km east of the fortress may hint at the presence of civilian settlement around the natural springs here which were the source of the fortress water supply.

The Port

The incorporation of vast tracts of new territory into the province in the early 70s of the first century involved a forward move in the disposition of the legions in Britain, and it was undoubtedly Chester's location at the head of a navigable estuary, together with its possession of a fine natural harbour, that caused it to be chosen as the site for the new fortress needed in the north-west. Access to the sea was important to the high command in a number of ways: for the mounting of combined land and sea operations, such as those which played such a prominent role in Agricola's campaigns in Scotland; the logistical support of land forces by the fleet; the import of raw materials needed for the construction and maintenance of the fortress, such as metals from North Wales especially lead and copper; the movement of men and manufactured goods, such as pottery, brick and tile and metal goods, to the garrisons of the outlying auxiliary forces in its command area and later northwards to the west end of Hadrian's Wall and the Antonine Wall; and, most importantly, for the importation of the vast quantities of foodstuffs and other materials required by the legion, especially grain, which it would have been impossible to obtain locally and which it was far easier to transport by water than overland. At both of the other permanent legionary bases, Caerleon and York, there is evidence that grain was shipped in from as far afield as the Mediterranean, and the same was probably true at Chester. Other commodities unobtainable locally were also imported from abroad, such as wine and olive oil from Gaul and Spain, as were specialist forms of manufactured goods such as pottery and glassware from the Rhineland.

In the later Roman period patrol vessels would have operated out of a naval base at Chester to keep watch for sea-raiders, while the military command would have had access to valuable intelligence about the political situation amongst the tribes both north of Hadrian's Wall and across the Irish Sea from the independent seafaring merchants who called regularly at Deva. The truth of this is well illustrated by a passage in Tacitus' *Agricola* 24, where he tells us that his famous father-in-law acquired much information about the approaches and harbours of Ireland from this source. There is no evidence for the existence of a fleet for the western seaboard independent of the *classis Britannica*. Yet it might be thought strange that stamped bricks and tiles of the latter, so numerous at sites along the south-east coast, are totally absent in the west, where the volume of naval activity

Ill V.10 Tombstone of *optio* who died in a shipwreck.
(Copyright Chester City Council, Grosvenor Museum)

must have been quite considerable. Perhaps the evidence is there but simply has not been recognised. How would one know, for example, whether the stamp 'CLIV' on a brick was merely the batch number '154' or an abbreviation for *Cl[assis Iv[ernica]* (the *Oceanus Ivernicus* being the Roman name for the Irish Sea)? Certainly in the fourth century, when naval defences along the west coast were strengthened with the addition of Saxon Shore-type forts at Cardiff, Lancaster and Holyhead, Chester would have been the obvious head-quarters for such a separate naval command. By this period, though, it was common for the constituent squadrons or flotillas of a fleet to be named after the forts where they were based. Thus, in this period, if not a *Classis Ivernica*, there could well have been a flotilla known as the *Classis Devae* at Chester. We have but a single inscription from Chester with a naval connection and it also demonstrates the dangers of sea travel. This is the tombstone of a man (his name does not survive) serving in the century of Lucilius Ingenuus and awaiting promotion from *optio* to centurion who died in a shipwreck — *naufragio periit* — before his new rank could be confirmed (Ill V.10).

Post-Roman changes in the course and flow of the Dee estuary, coupled with land reclama-tion schemes, now render it difficult to envisage the port of Roman Chester. The harbour lay to the west of the fortress where the erosive power of the Dee at the end of the last Ice Age had gouged out the large bowl-shaped area now known as the Roodee, just before the river opens out into its broad estuary. This spot is now occupied by the racecourse, a recreational facility formed out of land which had already been reclaimed from the sea by

Ill V.11 Best preserved section of the so-called 'quay wall' beside the Roodee

the middle of the sixteenth century. The modern visitor's comprehension of how this area once looked is further impeded by its total visual separation from the general course of the Dee by the embankment for the Grosvenor Bridge at the south end and the nineteenth-century railway viaduct at the other.

What has traditionally been regarded as the sole surviving feature of Deva's harbour is the so-called Roman 'quay wall' which lies at the eastern edge of the Roodee below and a few metres in advance of the medieval City Walls. Although only a comparatively short section is now visible opposite the junction of Blackfriars Lane with Nun's Road, observations during building and engineering works in the late nineteenth and early twentieth centuries enabled it to be traced northwards as far as the Water Gate, a distance in excess of 200 m. At the south end of the visible portion, the wall appears to be turning to the south-east to follow the contours of the mouth of the substantial inlet or valley which once existed in this area. The wall was about 2.4 m thick and was constructed of large blocks of sandstone 0.30–0.40 m high and up to 1.2 m in length bonded together with high quality mortar, the whole backed by at least 1.5 m of concrete. The extant length of wall survives to an average height of 1 m above the present surface of the Roodee but it originally rose much higher than this, as is demonstrated by the best preserved section (now enclosed by railings) where there is nearly 3 m of upstanding masonry (Ill V.11). Furthermore, explorations at this spot in 1884 followed the wall down to a depth of 4.60 m, where there was an offset course. Excavation below this level was prevented by the ingress of water, but the wall clearly carried on down for some considerable distance and calculations suggest that in order to obtain a secure base there would have been at least another 3 m below this point. The nineteenth-century exploration also demonstrated the presence of pilaster-like buttresses on its outer face.

The quay wall was obviously a very substantial feat of engineering, and in terms of the quantities of stone used alone it was the equivalent of more than half the entire circuit of the fortress curtain wall. But did it actually function as a quay where ships could be loaded and unloaded? There is in fact persuasive evidence to suggest that it did not. First, close to the spot where the railway passes over the modern river channel, excavations to allow the insertion of foundations for a new gasometer in 1885 struck the ancient river bed, here consisting of boulder clay covered by 0.30–0.40 m of coarse gravel, at a depth of about 6 m below ground level (roughly equivalent to 0.00 m OD). Lying on this were lengths of oak timbers averaging 0.30 m in diameter and in excess of 3 m in length, some of which had a point at one end encased in an iron sheath and set around with concrete (Ill V.12). These were clearly the piles for some substantial structure such as a wharf or jetty, and close by was found the 2-m-deep trench into which they had been set. That they were Roman is clear not only from their similarity to piles found used in Roman structures elsewhere, particularly bridges, but also from the fact that they were surrounded by a mass of Roman material which included bricks and tiles, samian ware and other types of pottery, and an ingot of lead bearing a cast inscription with consular dates indicating its manu-facture in AD 74 from ore mined in the territory of Deceangli (roughly modern Flintshire). A wall with a stepped northern face found a few years later a little to the south, if Roman, could have been a replacement for the earlier timber landing stage.

Contemporary writers linked the dis-coveries at the gas works with similar timbers found outside the Water Gate in 1874, also at a considerable depth and associated with Roman material, to suggest that they represented opposite ends of a single large landing stage ex-tending from the eastern shoreline of the Roodee for a distance of about 350 m. This idea later fell into disfavour, in part at least owing to the acceptance of the

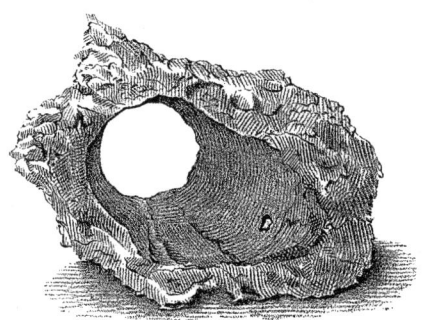

IMPRESSION OF IRON SHOE OF OAK PILE.

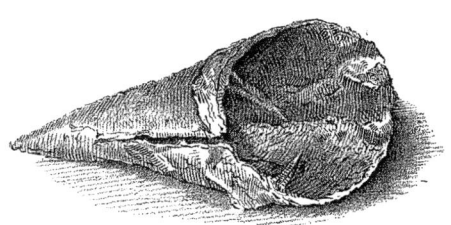

POINTED END OF IRON SHOE.

OTHER REMAINS,
FOUND AT THE ROODEYE, 1885.

Ill V.12 Drawings of iron shoes from timber piles found in 1885 during construction of a gasometer. (*J Chester Archaeol Soc* new ser **1**, 1887, facing 80.)

interpretation of the wall running along the east edge of the Roodee as a quay. Consequently, the gas works timbers were instead seen as belonging to a landing stage projecting out from the west bank of the river, the assumption being that the channel in the Roman period lay further east than it does today. There are, however, obvious difficulties with this interpretation. Firstly, there is a steep cliff on the west side of the river at this point and, secondly, any goods offloaded at this point would have to be transported by cart on a roundabout journey through what is now Curzon Park and Handbridge, across the bridge over the Dee, and then up the steep slope leading to the south gate of the fortress. Secondly, there is no evidence for any form of Roman installation on this side of the river.

The results of recent research into sea levels in the Roman period in general and tidal conditions in the Roodee area in particular suggest that the Victorian writers were correct in their interpretation of the gas works/Water Gate timbers, and this in turn has important implications for the 'quay wall'. At the time that Chester was founded, sea levels are thought to have been somewhat lower than it is today. The precise level is much debated but this need not concern us here as there is evidence from Chester itself sufficient for our purposes. The timbers found outside the Water Gate in 1874 mentioned above were discovered during excavations for the laying of a new main sewer at the foot of the City Walls. Several hundred metres to the south, beneath the race course track and at a spot on the far side of the mouth of the large inlet south-west of the fortress, these same excavations encountered a Roman burial. The grave contained two skeletons, an adult and a child, which the accompanying tombstone identified as Flavius Callimorphus and his son or nephew Serapion. Amongst the grave goods was a coin of Domitian (AD 81–96). The grave was 1.80 m deep, and it is possible to work out from the information recorded that its floor lay at a level about 3.5m OD. The position and depth of this grave is very important because it shows that this area was dry land in the early Roman period and that there had already been considerable silt deposition along the east side of the Roodee by the time that Chester was founded.

It is also clear both from this discovery and levels recorded in more recent excavations near the Old Dee Bridge that even the highest tide in the Roman era is unlikely to have reached a level over 4.5 m OD. Ordinary tides may have averaged around 4 m, receding to 1.5–2.0 m at the ebb. As the sort of sea-going vessels using the harbour had a draft of about 1.5 m when laden it is obvious that they could only have approached the eastern shore of the Roodee and the 'quay wall' at periods of high tide and even then only in part because of the build-up of silt in front of its southern half. This would have been most inconvenient for the military authorities given the volume of materials with which the port had to cope. The solution was the erection of the structure to which the gas works and Water Gate timbers belonged, a landing stage projecting from the fortress side of the Roodee basin into the deepest part of the river channel — the outer bend lying close to the opposite bank — which allowed ships to dock and cargoes to be transferred under most, if not all, tidal conditions (Ill V.13).

What then of the 'quay wall'? While the possibility of ships actually tying up against it seems unlikely, it has been suggested that it was still able to function as a quay by means of additional jetties projecting out at right angles. However, the top of the best preserved

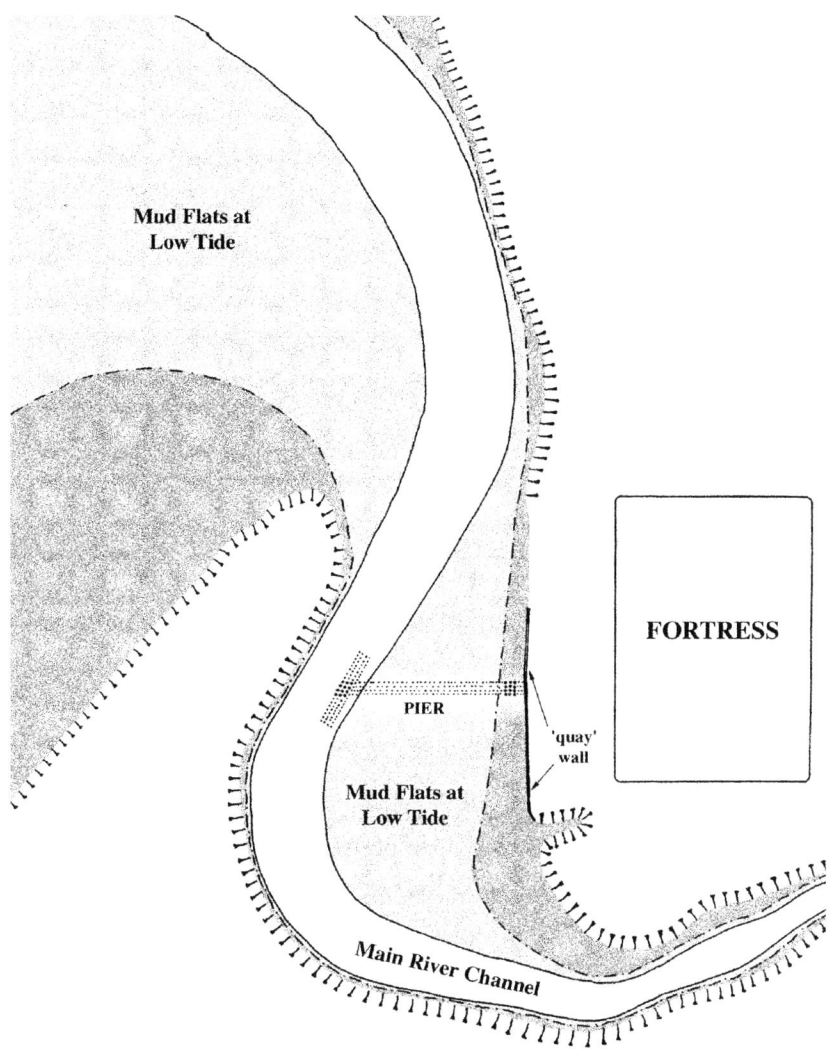

III V.13 Possible condition of harbour area in late first century AD: map showing extensive mud flats and position of timber pier. (Not to scale)

section of the wall lies at around 11.00 m OD, and it has the appearance of having risen still further originally, whereas the deck of an averaged sized sea-going vessel of the period would have lain about 2 m above the water line, the equivalent of *c* 6.00 m OD under optimum local river conditions. Having a quayside 5 m higher than deck level is clearly a nonsense. So, if not a quay, what was the function of the 'quay wall'? Excavation has shown that Roman ground level immediately east of the City Walls lies at *c* 13.00 m OD, and it seems quite feasible that the wall was carried up for another 2 m to reach this level. Perhaps, therefore, in the same way that the City Walls here have enabled the ground behind them to be built up and levelled, the 'quay wall' was constructed as a revetment to enable the steep natural slope down to the Roodee to be reclaimed and terraced so as to increase building space. Yet building a wall 2.4 m thick and at least 12 m high (requiring around 30,000 blocks of stone each weighing around half a tonne for a 200-m length) to reclaim a strip of land no more than 5 m wide seems an effort out of all proportion to the gain. Furthermore, there was plenty of spare land available for building to the south of the fortress.

For a work of this scale, there is only one possible explanation left — that its purpose was principally, if not exclusively, one of defence. The erection of walls around legionary suburbs in the later Roman period is a phenomenon found at a number of fortresses, including those at Mogontiacum (Mainz), Aquincum (Budapest) and Novae (Stuklen). In our case, the intention was presumably to protect the western sector of the *canabae*, which, evidence suggests, was the wealthiest section of the extramural settlement. This would not, however, have entailed the demolition of the western fortress wall, for that is known to have been maintained and repaired into the fourth century. The date of the 'quay wall' is unknown but it is very probably later than a group of late first- or early second-century burials discovered close behind it. Its course beyond the Water Gate is unknown but it undoubtedly continued along the frontage of the large bath building immediately to the north. An eastward return, running back to link up with fortress defences, would have been required to close off the north side of the defended enceinte and this might have lain shortly beyond the baths. However, there is reason to believe that it followed the same line as the section of the medieval town wall which runs from Morgan's Mount (close to the site of the fortress north-west angle tower) down to Bonewaldesthorne's Tower at the north-west corner of the circuit (Ill V.14).

The present City Walls stand on top of and slightly back from an older wall, a situation frequently found along those parts of the walls where the medieval and Roman defences coincide. Much of the lower wall is obscured by the accumulation of soil against its outer face but varying types of masonry are apparent, including sections built of large blocks like those found in the 'quay wall'. This suggests that either it was built with whatever materials were to hand, with little care for style or appearance, or that it represents successive phases of construction and repair. Partway along this sector stands Pemberton's Parlour, in origin a medieval tower once known as the Goblin Tower, which was partially demolished and rebuilt in 1701 with its upper part being reconstructed again in 1894. It is the relationship between the base of this tower and the lower wall just mentioned that is potentially very significant. The towers of the medieval circuit were designed so that approximately half of their diameter projected forward of the curtain wall for obvious

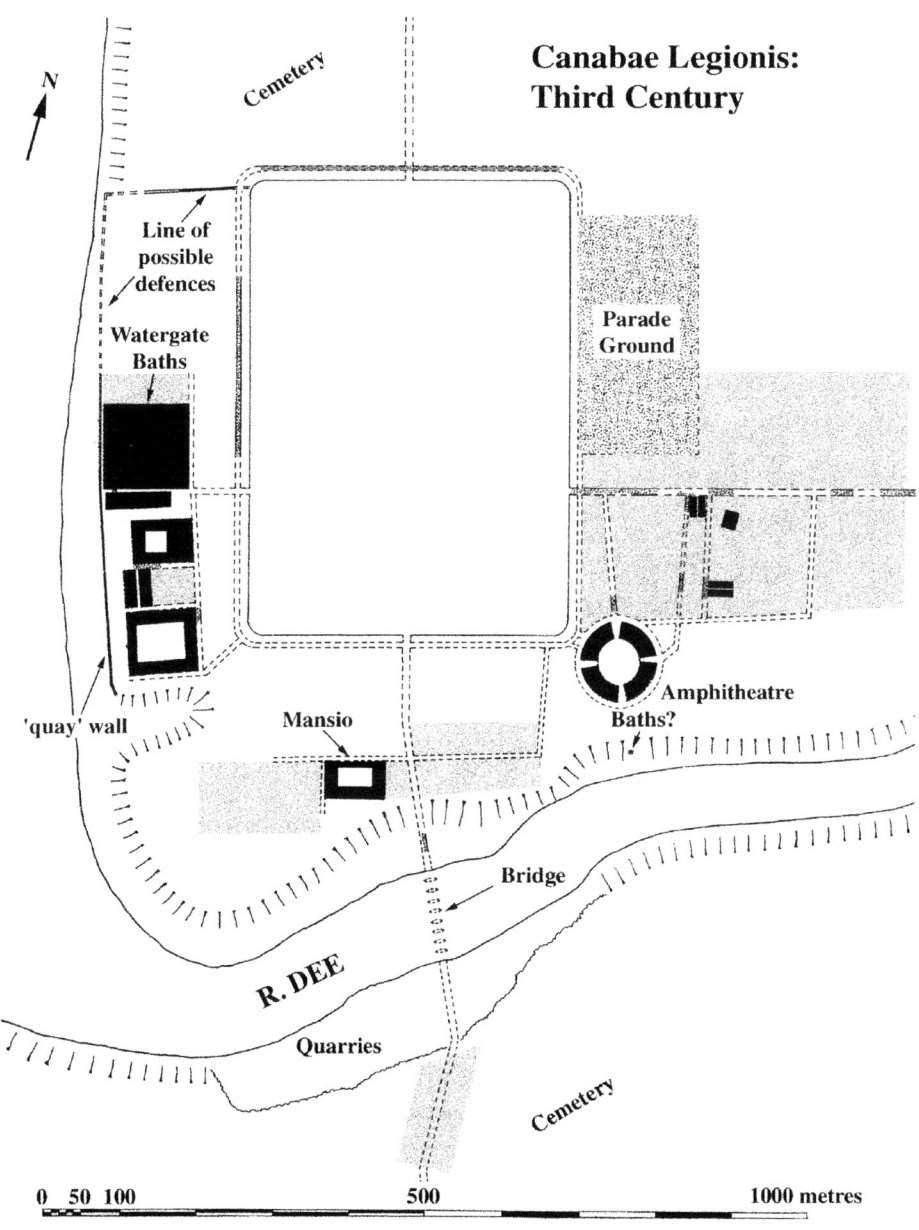

**Canabae Legionis:
Third Century**

Cemetery

N

Line of
possible
defences

Watergate
Baths

Parade
Ground

'quay' wall

Mansio

Amphitheatre
Baths?

Bridge

R. DEE

Quarries

Cemetery

0   50 100   500   1000 metres

Ill V.14 Western sector of *canabae* with 'quay wall' re-interpreted as part of late defensive circuit.
(Scale 1/10 000)

defensive reasons, and this is precisely the relationship which exists between the Goblin Tower and the existing City Walls and also between the latter and Bonewaldesthorne's Tower further west. Yet the lower wall is almost flush with the front of the base of the Goblin Tower and in fact shows every indication of having been partially removed to make way for the tower. Despite much rebuilding, the Goblin Tower must still stand on its original foundations. Thus, the lower wall must be earlier. This could represent a stretch of the original walls erected in the late twelfth–early thirteenth centuries with the work above and the accompanying towers replacing it a century later. Then again, the patchwork character of the visible facing might suggest a date in the late Anglo-Saxon period when Chester was again becoming a major military centre as well as a thriving port. Yet, the similarity between the relationship of the two phases of wall in this sector and that which exists elsewhere along the circuit between the fortress wall and medieval City Walls is so striking as to suggest the possibility that the lower wall might in fact be Roman in origin. If so, then it would constitute the eastward return of the 'quay wall', following a logical course for the northern defences of the western suburbs by linking up with the north-west corner of the fortress.

The course of the proposed circuit of defences beyond the southern end of the extant portion of the 'quay wall' can only be conjectural. The latter does begin to turn into the mouth of the neighbouring large inlet, and a logical solution would have been for it to carry on turning so as to link up with the south-west angle of the fortress. No trace of such was found when the latter was examined in the 1960s but this could be explained by the existence of a gap to accommodate a gate at the point of junction. The area thus enclosed would have amounted to 12.5 ha. It is worth noting in passing, however, that a wall of similar character to the 'quay wall' once ran along the frontage of the river to the west of the Old Dee Bridge. If — and it is a big if — this was also Roman then this may indeed have been a quay. Alternatively, and this is an even more startling possibility, it could have been a continuation of the 'quay wall' which would mean that the land south of the fortress was also included within the defended area, which would thus have totalled something approaching 48 ha. If so, then the line followed by the medieval City Walls, beyond as well as within the fortress, would have been established in the late Roman rather than the Norman period as is usually assumed.

The port of Chester is no more. But when next you look out across the green sward of the Roodee, where now Mammon is worshipped and everyone is seeking their own swift Pegasus, remember that this part of Chester was once under Neptune's sway.

Further Reading

Brock, E P L 1888   The age of the walls of Chester, with references to recent discussions. *J Chester Archaeol Soc* new ser **2**, 40–97

Mason, D J P 1977   The extramural area in: Strickland, T J & Davey, P J eds. New evidence for Roman Chester. Liverpool University, 29–40

Mason, D J P 1987   Chester: the *canabae legionis*. *Britannia* **18**, 143–68

Mason, D J P 1988a   The Roman site at Heronbridge, near Chester, Cheshire: aspects of civilian settlement in the vicinity of legionary fortresses in Britain and beyond. *Archaeol J* **145**, 123–5 7

Mason, D J P 1988b   *Prata legionis* in Britain. *Britannia* **19**, 163–89

Shrubsole, G W1887   The traffic between Deva and the coast of North Wales in the Roman period. *J Chester Archaeol Soc* new ser **1**, 76–90

Thompson, F H 1965   *Roman Cheshire*. Chester: Cheshire Community Council. (History of Cheshire **1**)

VI: Tales from the Tomb
Sculpture in Roman Chester

by M Henig MA, DPhil, DLitt, FSA

A new study of the sculpture of Roman Chester, much of it funerary in character and presumably incorporated in late Roman repairs to the north wall of the fortress where it was disengaged in the late nineteenth century, has confirmed its unique importance for the study of sculpture workshops in Roman Britain and more generally for its iconographic interest. This is the theme of my paper 'Chester and the art of the Twentieth Legion' (Henig 1999) and the full results will be published in a forthcoming fascicule of the *Corpus Signorum Imperii Romani* (now in press).

Amongst the discrete groups which can be seen are the simple tongue-like panels of the first-century tombstones of Legion II *Adiutrix*, sometimes with astrological symbols. The majority of the funerary monuments are, however, later, for the most part dating from the third century. Some of those of soldiers, like the centurion Marcus Aurelius Nepos who is shown with his wife, the *optio* Caecilius Avitus or the *imaginifer* Aurelius Diogenes, are surprisingly inept. However, this is probably not the result of their late date, as a contemporary altar dedicated to the *genius loci* by the military tribune Flavius Longus and his son Longinus is superbly detailed, following a remarkably consistent tradition of work beginning with Twentieth Legion distance slabs from the Antonine Wall and continuing with a relief from Lanchester and the famous altar found in Chester in the seventeenth century and now in the Ashmolean Museum, dedicated to Jupiter Tanarus by a *princeps* of the legion in AD 154. Presumably first-rate sculptors were hard to attract to remote stations, and it was only the legionary legate and his immediate circle who could provide the incentive regularly to attract talent from afar.

The range of subject matter is wide and the stones tell us a great deal about the inhabitants of the fortress. A relief showing a Sarmatian horseman holding a *draco* standard, is a reminder of a foreign element amongst the troops stationed here. One of an important group of banquet tombstones is enlivened by unusual additions. The feasting horseman Aurelius Lucianus is shown with his armour hanging on the wall behind him and accompanied in front by a servant holding a trophy, the head of an enemy. Was he a Celt or a Thracian tribesman like Caecilius Donatus? The latter's stele was, however, more conventional, giving no sign of a bloodthirsty career. The best of these banquet tombstones belong to civilians, several of them with names suggestive of an oriental origin. The stele of Callimorphus and a boy with the theophoric name Serapion was found in the nineteenth century *in situ* with both skeletons present and wealth and status guaranteed by a gold ring, now apparently lost. A second name recalling a deity is that of Curatia Di(o)nysia, who dines beneath hanging swags on which perch soul-birds, as does Fesonia Severina. The small girls Restita and Martia have a pecten shell behind them as does a lady on another stone; these shells probably symbolise the seas over which the departed soul must pass to the Blessed Isles. We can relate these stones to an altar tombstone showing a child, sleeping rather than dining. On each side is a bird standing on a block. Such blocks support the feet of Callimorphus' couch and that of one of the woman with the pecten shell. The birds pecking at a bunch of grapes allude to the wine of life and the saving power of Bacchus/ Dionysus.

It is noteworthy how many of the finest tombstones at Chester were memorials to wealthy women, which strongly suggest that in the third century, perhaps in particular towards the middle of the century, Chester acquired many of the features of a town. Of key interest are two stones, one showing a woman holding a mirror and the other a woman with a parrot, the bird of Bacchus, in each case accompanied by her maid. A third stele depicts a woman holding a hare, symbolising fecundity. Idiosyncrasies of this group include rich draperies and hands with fingers of exaggerated length.

All human life and death is here on the Chester gravestones, from the masons' tools showing the monument had been formally dedicated *sub ascia* (under the adze), perhaps in the owner's lifetime, to the guardian lions which will protect it from evil forces. There are a number of figures of Attis, the vegetation deity who died for love of the Great Mother and some believed was resurrected each year. Two reliefs of this 'dying god' ornamented one grand monument. A superb pediment from another built tomb has at its centre a Minerva mask conflated with a head of Neptune, the former a protective symbol against the Evil Eye but the latter indicating the voyage to the Isles of the Blessed, as do several representations of Neptune's retinue of tritons. Neptune-Medusa is best known as the central emblem on the pediment of the Flavian Temple of Sulis Minerva at Bath. Was this a later copy of that sculpture?

Other sculpture on built tombs showed scenes of myth: Lycurgus, Bacchus' adversary (surely doomed for his *hubris*), and Actaeon, who was turned into a stag by Diana for seeing her naked and then torn to pieces by his own hounds. On the other hand Hercules is depicted rescuing Hesione (from a sea monster), a clear image of superhuman salvation, while Adonis, perishing of a mortal wound beneath a carob tree, is the type of a 'dying god' resurrected each year in the spring vegetation. A cupid fishing represents the felicity of the soul, while hounds chasing stags more ambiguously represent both sudden death and the field sports in which the deceased hoped to indulge in the other world. A vegetal scroll on three adjoining blocks, inhabited by birds and flowers is not purely formal, bringing to mind as it does the soul, new life and the spring *rosalia* festival when the graves of the beloved dead were decked with roses.

The overwhelming impression given by these stones is optimistic. They show individuals proud of their past lives and facing the future with equanimity, looking forward to another life of plenty and of pleasure, under the protection of beneficent gods. As everyone who has worked on them for any length of time has realised, there is no collection like them in Britain and few with their range elsewhere in the western provinces of the empire. Indeed the Chester tombstones are of international importance.

It is thus very regrettable that many of them are badly stored, dirty, inaccessible and in some cases badly in need of sensitive conservation, and it is very much to be hoped that the present situation can soon be remedied, at the least by modern, adequate storage but ideally by a gallery large enough to display this wonderful collection to full advantage.

Bibliography

Henig, M 1999   Chester and the art of the Twentieth Legion. *In*: Medieval archaeology, art and architecture at Chester. (*British Archaeol Assoc Conf Trans* **22**), 1–15

VII: Where have all the Soldiers gone?
Some Thoughts on the Presence and Absence of Soldiers in Fourth-Century Chester

by B Hoffmann MA, DPhil, AIFA

The problem of recognition

A reading of the 1994 publication on Saxon Chester soon brings home the problems of this period. The Saxon layers dating to the ninth–tenth century are characterised by Simon Ward as follows: 'The basic relationship shared by all contexts identified as Saxon on the sites under consideration in this volume is that they lay in the stratigraphical sequence between the frequently more easily dated Roman and medieval levels.' (Ward *et al* 1994, 3–4). Given the fact that large-scale building in Roman Chester stopped in the third century it is tempting likewise to characterise the fourth-century occupation as being represented by the features lying between the recognisably earlier Roman layers and identifiable later, Saxon, structures. Unfortunately, the paucity of dating evidence is sometimes such that it is hard to tell what is late Roman and what Dark Age or Mercian.

In the past most efforts have rightly been focused on disentangling the often complicated earlier history of Chester, especially the date of its foundation and the plan of the fortress in the second and third centuries AD, and in reviewing the material for this paper it was surprising how little evidence we are actually dealing with. By the fourth century the Romans had a lot of good quality buildings from earlier periods they could continue to use. Evidence from elsewhere, for example Carnuntum, shows that late Roman occupation in fortresses often involved the adaptation of these existing buildings rather than the building of new ones. In a way this is unsurprising, as the practice continues today. For example, there is no twentieth-century cathedral in Chester because the old one is still perfectly serviceable, given some necessary changes to make it suitable for modern usage, like installing central heating, a cafe and a bookshop. It seems therefore not impossible to predict similar behaviour by the Romans with respect to their upstanding buildings.

A further complicating factor in the reconstruction of late Roman Chester is the diminishing size of the legions and with them often the size of the attached settlements. It can therefore not be ruled out that we have to expect much smaller numbers of people living in and around Chester.

Structural evidence
The defences
Thompson (1965, 29) assumed in the 1960s that the western defences of the fortress were destroyed shortly after the repairs to the north wall, which he dated to c AD 300 (for a late Saxon/early medieval date for these repairs, *see* now LeQuesne *et al* 1999, 120–1; 146–8). This would suggest an early end to the fortress as a defensible structure. This conflicts, however, with the historical evidence, which shows that in 893/4 the Danes were able to hold out against the Saxons inside the fortress for two days. Strickland has also convincingly argued that the slighting mentioned by Thompson was more likely to have occurred when the City Walls were extended to the Dee in the medieval period (Strickland in Ward *et al* 1994, 8–10). At St John Street Mason (1994–5, 13) argued that the defences collapsed and had then been rebuilt in the period AD 250–300.

If Thompson and Mason are correct, then in the fourth century the fortress area would have been protected by a recently refurbished wall, although this gives us little indication as to the character of the settlement inside.

The *principia*
Very little of the *principia* has been excavated, but from what we know it seems that it was refloored in the fourth century (Carrington ed 1994, 34). This paving appears to have extended over most of the building, as Ward seems to have found patches in the south range (1988, 15). He also argued that this extensive paving might be an indicator that the headquarters building continued in intensive use.

As to the end of the building he remarks (1988, 28): 'In conclusion, therefore, these [latest] pits are possibly evidence for a period of occupation at some date around the end of the fourth century or later. This occupation could have been in the still-standing south range of the *principia* or in lighter timber structures on the site of it. If it was in the *principia*, then it was probably a very different sort of occupation from that which the building had enjoyed earlier in its life. It is clear, however, that when this period of occupation ended, an organised demolition and site clearance was carried out. One important effect of the demolition and levelling of the Roman building was to raise the ground level by up to 1.5 m above the adjacent road surfaces. This seems to have occurred on the sites of all the major Roman buildings in the centre of the fortress'.

It cannot, therefore, be assumed that the *principia* was still fully functional throughout the fourth century and the question of whether it contained a church as Strickland and Thacker argue (Strickland in Ward *et al* 1994, 11) must for the moment remain open.

The Elliptical Building, the granaries and the other store buildings
The elaborate Elliptical Building also has rebuilding evidence dating to the fourth century (Mason 2000,143–9), while Ward (1988, 15; Ward *et al* 1994, 43) mentions fourth-century sandstone paving in the large store buildings in the *retentura*. Strickland and Ward believe that especially the store building to the north of the Elliptical Building continued to remain standing and even to acquire a number of timber structures in its north yard in the latest Roman period. Also still standing and functioning was the granary in Hunter Street (in Ward *et al* 1994, 12).

In fact, the only store buildings that were demolished in the course of the fourth century were apparently the granaries in Commonhall Street. With regard to these, Thompson recorded that they did not contain much dating evidence. However, he then went on to say:

> Large-scale demolition was reflected by a consistent layer of broken roof tiles between the granaries and in the spaces between the sleeper walls. From this layer and above it were recovered coins of the late third and the early fourth centuries [Carausius and Constantius], suggesting that by then the granaries were no longer being used for their original purpose. Two ventilators were also filled with a rough masonry blocking, unfortunately undated but perhaps connected with the conversion of the granaries to some other purpose during the Roman period. (Thompson 1965, 39).

The presence of roofing debris between the sleeper walls implies that somebody had taken up the raised stone floor and that, as Thompson concluded, the granaries had ceased to operate as such at some point after the end of the third century AD. However, it also implies that there were still people living inside the fortress who were willing and able to conduct large rebuilding programmes necessitating the removal of the flagging (perhaps to re-pave the *principia* or the *retentura*?). The presence of the broken tiles may attest a later accidental collapse of the granary roof, although a controlled demolition can also not be ruled out.

These features remind one of a very similar sequence at the granaries in Birdoswald (Wilmott 1997, 110–28), where the roof collapse and the filling in of the sleeper walls represented the first stage of a late and post-Roman sequence of events that saw the conversion of the granaries into a dwelling house and eventually a timber hall, although no similar structures were reported at Commonhall Street.

The fortress baths
The main fortress baths appear to have remained functional until the end of the fourth century (Mason in Ward *et al* 1994, 18; *forthcoming*). The small bath house to the south of the Elliptical Building also remained standing well into the Saxon period, suggesting that the fortress continued to enjoy a comparatively high standard of living, as it was certainly able to provide bathing facilities for a large number of people (Mason 2000, 150–1).

The barracks
At Crook Street and Goss Street, as well as probably in Abbey Green (Strickland in Ward *et al* 1994, 12), it seems that the barracks and the centurions' quarters survived well into the fourth century, with a layer of paving representing the very latest Roman activity, which is overlain by the collapse of the structures (Ward *et al* 1994, 22, 29 and 70).

On the other hand Thompson stressed that the barrack buildings in the Deanery Field (directly adjoining Abbey Green) were systematically demolished at the end of the third century (Thompson 1965, 36). It seems therefore reasonable to expect that at least one, perhaps two, cohort blocks were no longer operative in late Roman period.

At Northgate Brewery the situation was slightly more complicated. The latest recognisable barrack buildings of the old style were demolished at the end of the third century, but this appears to have been followed by a late timber phase about which very little is known and the dating of which cannot be refined beyond the 'after the end of the third century' of the preceding phase (Ward & Strickland 1978, 26–7). The surviving features consisted of a few post holes, a rubble spread, a paving over an earlier cess pit and perhaps an adjoining hearth. Dug into the rubble was a pit containing residual pottery and a broken sword. This last item cannot easily be fitted into a civilian context and might be one of our best indicators that there were armed personnel at that time in Chester. Given the publication of the Saxon remains in Chester, which saw the re-attribution of the other late timber buildings at similar sites to the Saxon period (Ward *et al* 1994), it may be worthwhile to re-examine the sequence of this site as well. But until then the sword remains a candidate for interpretation as a late Roman artefact.

The *vicus*

Thompson (1965, 45) assumed that most of the *vicus* had been destroyed by the end of the second century AD. However, he noted that the then very recent excavations at 46–50 Foregate Street in 1961 had produced walls from a late third- or fourth-century building, while to the north of the site a surface sealing pottery of the late third and fourth century was noted.

More recent work has shown that the so-called *mansio* in Castle Street continued into the fourth century (Mason 1980, 4 and 23–5). The Phase III building had been destroyed by fire at the end of the third century and then rebuilt. The later activity on the site can be summarised as follows: at some time in the first half of the fourth century, perhaps *c* 330, the passage way separating two blocks was enclosed by crudely built walling and new surfaces were laid. About the middle of the century the second well, which had been kept in commission, was backfilled to ground level and a large quantity of masonry derived from demolished walling was used to top up the filling of the first well, which had sunk owing to compaction. It is possible that these operations mark the end of the occupation on the site, but levels which may have provided evidence to the contrary could well have been removed by nineteenth-century levelling. Mason also stresses the absence of any material dating to after the middle of the fourth century.

The amphitheatre had last been rebuilt in the 270s with stone paving slabs being laid in the arena. The abandonment of the structure is dated to the mid-fourth century (Thompson 1976, 172, 179). It is to be hoped that future work may be able to refine the history of this structure.

Discussion

The status of Chester in the fourth century

In summary, by the beginning of the fourth century Chester was still full of substantial buildings with signs of recent repairs outside but especially within the fortress walls. There is enough fourth-century pottery to prove continued occupation. A lot of sites, however, appear to show a complete absence of archaeological material dating to the second half of the fourth century or later, suggesting a dramatic reduction in settlement size. The coin list also shows the typical peaks and troughs until the 360s, when it suddenly declines, suggesting relatively 'normal' conditions in Chester until the middle of the fourth century (Shotter 1998–9, 45; Carrington ed 1994, 29).

In addition to this we also find a number of Mediterranean and continental imports on the site (Carrington ed 1994, 53). The continental pottery, particularly Mayen ware, is to be expected in a settlement this size; the Mediterranean imports are, however, much less common.

Also unusual is the type of building surviving. One would have expected the bath buildings and the granaries to survive for a while, as they offered amenities that could be used by civilians as well as the military. In Chester however, we have a substantial survival of large store buildings combined with the destruction of several of the granaries.

This raises some questions as to the nature of the population inhabiting the fortress, especially the problem of the continued presence of the legion. Strickland (1984, 30–5) argued that the widespread evidence for demolition, then dated to the end of the third century, indicated that the legion left Chester about that time and that the site probably became a civilian town operating as the capital of one of the late Roman British provinces, perhaps with some small military component, while Carrington (ed 1994, 29) argued that the decline of the coinage after the 360s might indicate that the army left Chester only in the later fourth century.

The latest evidence for Legion XX *Valeria Victrix* at Chester consists of tiles giving the legion the title *Deciana*, an honour bestowed by the emperor Trajan Decius (249–251) in the early third century AD (Carrington ed 1994, 29). We know of a third-century detachment under or at least incorporating one Aurelius Cervianus, which is commemorated on a roundel probably found in Gaul (now in the Cabinet de France). By 255 this or another vexillation is attested at Mainz in Germany (CIL **13**, 6780), while by *c* 260 a joint vexillation of XX *Valeria Victrix* and II *Augusta* was operating on the Danube and in Pannonia (CIL **3**, 3228). It has been argued that these vexillations were cut off from their parent units when Postumus rebelled against Gallienus in 260, although we are lacking positive proof (Coello 1996, 18). There is also an altar to Cocidius from Bankhead set up by men of Legion XX *Valeria Victrix*. The latest evidence for the legion are coins struck by Carausius for the unit between 287 and 293 (RIC, Carausius 82, 83, 275: Le Quesne *et al* 1999, 6; Carrington ed 1994, 29).

The later history of the legion remains therefore debatable: it may have continued for a while without commemorating its name, or it may have been disbanded or destroyed. If the vexillations on the continent did not return, we have to assume that the unit was at least temporarily under-strength from the mid-third century AD. The legion does not appear to be mentioned in the *Notitia Dignitatum* (written in the late fourth century), although John Casey has raised the possibility that the Comitatensian unit of the *Victores Iuniores Brittanniciani* derived from the Legion XX *Valeria Victrix*, although Legion VI *Victrix* cannot be ruled out as a possible alternative (Casey 1990, 18). The identification of units mentioned in the *Notitia Dignitatum* with earlier units can be far from easy, given the fact that some of the name changes are substantial and hard to explain from the limited evidence available: for example Legion II *Italica* seems to have turned into the *Divitenses* and one or some of the Pannonian legions are listed as *Pannoniciani Seniores*.

The size of the late Roman legion

The possibility of the Legion XX operating under-strength has already been noted. This, however, raises another vexed question: the size of the later Roman legion. Most people agree that in the later Roman period we have to expect legionary units that were substantially smaller than the original 5000–6000 soldiers mentioned for the first and second centuries AD. Often vexillations (as well as specialists with the legion like the horsemen and the *lanciarii*) were split from the main body and never returned, or the original unit was allowed to run down in size. Following a set of numbers surviving in papyri from Egypt, the size for one of these later legions is usually given as about 1000 men (Carrington ed 1994, 29; Casey 1990, 14), equivalent to about a fifth or sixth of the original nominal strength of the fortress garrison. The scanty evidence, however, does not allow us to make any statements as to whether this size applied throughout the empire and if so, when it became the norm. It is theoretically possible that some of the older legions survived for a while with higher numbers.

Given the problems of the size, the next problem that needs addressing is the question of the accommodation of any military personnel. Until recently the accommodation of legionary soldiers in the early empire was usually assumed to be straightforward: soldiers inside the fortifications, women and children and other dependents outside. However, finds in auxiliary forts (for example in Vindolanda) in the last few years have shown that this situation might actually never have been quite so clear cut, but as a rule of thumb it still holds.

From the early third century onwards this situation changed: soldiers were now allowed to formally marry, and it is often assumed that this also meant that they were allowed to live with their wives, although this is nowhere stated in the surviving sources. The result would be a mixing of the two populations and therefore, finds with female associations (eg, mirrors: Lloyd-Morgan 1977), as well as children's toys and clothes, inside the fortress, and finds of military equipment outside the fortifications. Rather than discussing concentrations of finds, we should therefore turn to the question of space allocation.

The Chester fortress has long been recognised as unusually large. Whereas 'normal' legionary fortresses are about 20 ha in size, Chester was *c* 10% bigger, or 22.5 ha (Carrington ed 1994, 29). This size difference could be expressed by equating it with other sites: Chester had in the second century the same amount of space as a 'standard' legionary fortress plus the auxiliary forts of Vindolanda (1.46 ha) and Gelligaer II (1.18 ha) combined.

So when assessing the needs of a late Roman legion in Chester, perhaps reviewing the evidence from other late fortresses might shed some light on the problem. The fortress in Deutz, opposite Cologne, has long been assumed to be the base of the 1000-strong Legion XXII *Constantiniana Victrix* and later the base of the Legion II *Italica Divitensis*. In a recent article Maureen Carroll (1998) has drawn attention to the problems of this equation. The first unit is only known from its brick stamps and this is not a proof of residence, while the second one is known from the *Notitia Dignitatum*. However, Carroll has also drawn attention to the fact that the calculation of a thousand-strong unit is based on a reconstruction that assigns twelve barracks to centuries containing eighty soldiers each, giving space for 960 men, while the four central barracks were reserved for the administration and the officers' accommodation. As Carroll pointed out, this leaves no room for workshops, stores and stabling, even though cavalry equipment is known from the fortress. By comparison with other late Roman forts of similar size, therefore, it seemed to her much more likely that Deutz housed only a 500-strong unit, perhaps part of the legion.

Similarly the small fortress at Castrum Rauracense/Kaiseraugst near Basel has traditionally been identified as the main base for Legion I *Martia*. A recent reassessment (Fellmann 1998) has shown that this was only one of three known locations for the legion in the first half of the fourth century, the others being Oedenburg/Biesheim and Breisach further along the Rhine, which might again suggest a split unit.

So the comparison with newly built legionary fortresses (and other examples just tend to prove the point) show that we have very little understanding of the space needed by late Roman legions. However, given the size of Chester, there should have been no problem finding sufficient room for a late legion within the fortress, even with the reduction in residential accommodation caused by the demolition of some of the barracks.

The role of late Roman Chester

In fact what is in many ways surprising is not the partly destroyed barrack buildings — after all in Caerleon we also see the demolition of barrack blocks from the third century onwards — but the substantial effort to keep a large number of buildings well maintained and usable, which must have put a huge strain on the personnel in residence. The fact that the effort was made suggests that these buildings must have been important. Quite a number of them are interpreted as having started life as stores: their ground plan is often mirrored in buildings known from harbour areas in Ostia and elsewhere (eg Rickman 1971, figs 18 and 22), and this may suggest a role for Chester in the fourth century AD as a store base and transhipment point for goods to and from Britain. However, the fact that it was the granaries closest to the Dee that were destroyed suggests that these goods did not include grain, although there is little proof to link the surviving buildings with mining in the North Wales mountains. Transhipment and harbour facilities would also explain the Mediterranean imports in Chester. But harbour facilities even in the late Roman period do not always demand a military presence, so what positive proof for the presence of late Roman soldiers survives from Chester in the fourth century?

Very little military equipment from the early Roman period survived into the fourth century unchanged. Probably the least important change is the fact that soldiers were now wearing 'trousers' with their tunics. The swords were longer and worn on the left side, the shield is round and the helmet enclosed the face even more fully than the early Roman examples. These changes should allow us to identify late Roman soldiers easily in the material, especially the infantry equipment, which included long swords, javelins, round shields, helmets, perhaps arrows and bows and, most importantly, late Roman military belts and crossbow brooches (Bishop & Coulston 1993, 160–182).

However, while late Roman crossbow brooches are known from Chester, military belt fittings have not so far been encountered in the published material. As mentioned above, late Roman swords tended to be generally longer than the earlier *gladii*, and although easily identified among the military finds, they are only rarely encountered on settlement sites. In fact, most of the swords known so far come from the graves of Germanic mercenaries rather than from Roman fortifications. However, the sword from Northgate Brewery mentioned earlier remains a possible candidate (Ward & Strickland 1978, 26).

The identification of missile weapons is further complicated by the fact that javelin- and arrow heads from the fourth century AD, apart from the *barbuli* and the *plumbatae,* show little difference to earlier spears and javelins and therefore only rarely allow safe dating. Taking these caveats into account very little survives in Chester that can safely be identified as late Roman military equipment, but before discarding the possibility of a Roman military presence in Chester it has to be kept in mind that other late Roman sites such as Richborough and York have produced similarly low concentrations of late Roman military equipment.

Magnentius and the end of military occupation at Chester

After reviewing the evidence as it stands, we therefore have to say that while we have little positive proof to support a continued presence of the Legion XX *Valeria Victrix* in Chester there is even less to rule out such a presence until the 360s. All that remains for me now is to present a model that would explain the sudden decline of Chester in the later fourth century.

In the 350s Magnentius deposed Constans, the reigning emperor in the west. This usurpation culminated in the battle of Mursa, on the 28 September 351, between Magnentius and Constantius II. This battle had the reputation amongst the fourth-century historians of being the bloodiest battle in a century that has several other contenders for this title, including the battle of Adrianople twenty-seven years later. The 'official' figures speak of 50,000 casualties, all members of the Roman army. The Germanic invasions along the Rhine were probably a direct result, and the reduced overall manpower appears to have triggered a major restructuring of military forces, especially in the western empire. We know of substantial changes in the German units like Legion I *Martia* (Fellmann 1998) and possibly the Deutz garrison (Carroll 1998). Is it not more than likely that, if the Chester legion was not destroyed in the battle itself, it may very well have been sent elsewhere or amalgamated with other units? This would explain both the sudden drop in the coin list and the lack of the archaeological material after the middle of the fourth century as well, as the omission of the legion from the *Notitia Dignitatum.*

One last point needs mentioning. Carrington (ed 1994, 51) states that Gildas' reference to the martyrs Aaron and Julius in *legionum urbs*, could just as well refer to Chester as to Caerleon, as Gildas has been connected with the monastery of Bangor is Coed. If this is the case, two things stand out. First, Deva changed its name in the late Roman phase. In itself, this is nothing surprising as quite a few places appear to have undergone this change, amongst them Caerleon, which dropped the name Isca. The problem is one of inference, as it is tempting to link the new name with the continuing presence of the legion. However, this need not be the case, as we know that the legion in Caerleon was moved but the name nevertheless continued. So unfortunately, whichever way the location of Aaron and Julius eventually goes, it does not help with determining the status of Chester.

If we see the legion continuing in Chester or prefer to interpret it as a civilian place, we know from the archaeology that Chester continued into the Dark Ages (eg Ward *et al* 1994 and Mason 1985) and that it was important enough to attract high-status goods such as Mediterranean amphorae (Carrington ed 1994, 53), suggesting a more than usual importance for the place.

Bibliography

Bishop, M & Coulston, J C N 1993 — Roman military equipment. London: Batsford

Bridger, C & Gilles, K J eds 1998 — Spätrömische Befestigungsanlagen in den Rhein- und Donauprovinzen. Oxford: British Archaeological Reports. (BAR Int Ser **704**)

Carrington, P ed 1994 — The English Heritage book of Chester. London: Batsford

Carroll, M 1998 — Das spätrömische Militärlager Divitia in Köln-Deutz und seine Besatzungen. *In*: Bridger & Gilles eds, 49–55

Casey, P J 1990 — The legions in the later Roman empire. Cardiff: National Museum of Wales. (Fourth Annual Caerleon Lecture)

Coello, T 1996 — Unit sizes in the late Roman army. Oxford: British Archaeological Reports. (BAR Int Ser **645**)

CIL — *Corpus inscriptionum Latinarum*. Berlin: Royal Prussian Academy of Letters, 1863–

Fellmann, R 1998 — Spätrömische Festungen und Posten im Bereich der Legion I Martia. *In*: Bridger & Gilles eds, 95–103

LeQuesne, C *et al* 1999 — Excavations at Chester, the Roman and later defences, part 1: investigations 1978–1990. Chester City Council. (Chester Archaeol Excav Surv Rep **11**)

Lloyd-Morgan, G 1977 — Mirrors in Roman Chester. *J Chester Archaeol Soc* new ser **66**, 49–55

Mason, D J P 1980 — Excavations at Chester: 11–15 Castle Street and neighbouring sites 1974–8: a possible Roman posting house (*mansio*). Chester City Council. (Grosvenor Mus Archaeol Excav Surv Rep **2**)

Mason, D J P 1985 — Excavations at Chester, 26–42 Lower Bridge Street 1974–6: the Dark Age and Saxon periods. Chester City Council. (Grosvenor Mus Archaeol Excav Surv Rep **3**)

Mason, D J P 1994–5 — II: 'And the walls came tumbling down: excavations adjacent to the City Walls in St John Street 1988/9'. *J Chester Archaeol Soc* new ser **73**, 11–20

Mason, D J P 2000   Excavations at Chester, the Elliptical Building: an image of the
                           Roman world? Excavations in 1939 and 1963–9. Chester City Council.
                           (Chester Archaeol Excav Surv Rep **12**)

Mason, D J P   Excavations at Chester, the baths of the Roman fortress:
forthcoming   investigations 1732–1988. Chester City Council. (Chester Archaeol
                           Excav Surv Rep **13**)

Rickman, G E 1971   Roman granaries and store buildings. Cambridge U P

RIC   Mattingly, H *et al*. The Roman imperial coinage. London: Spink,
                           1923–

Shotter, D C A 1998–9   III: Chester, the evidence of Roman coin loss. *J Chester Archaeol Soc*
                           new ser **75**, 33–50

Strickland, T J 1984   Roman Chester. Nelson: Hendon

Thompson, F H 1965   Roman Chester. Chester: Cheshire Community Council. (History of
                           Cheshire **1**)

Thompson, F H 1976   The excavation of the Roman amphitheatre at Chester. *Archaeologia*
                           105, 127–239

Ward, S W 1988   Excavations at Chester, 12 Watergate Street 1985: Roman
                           headquarters building to medieval Row. Chester City Council.
                           (Grosvenor Mus Archaeol Excav Surv Rep **5**)

Ward, S W *et al* 1994   Excavations at Chester, Saxon occupation within the Roman fortress:
                           sites excavated 1978–1981. Chester City Council. (Archaeol Serv
                           Excav Surv Rep 7)

Ward, S W &   Excavations at Chester, Northgate Brewery 1974/5: a Roman
Strickland, T J 1978   centurion's quarters and barrack. Chester City Council. (Grosvenor
                           Mus Archaeol Excav Surv Rep **1**)

Wilmott, T 1997   Birdoswald. Excavations of a Roman fort on Hadrian's Wall and its
                           successor settlements: 1987–1992. London: English Heritage

VIII: The Construction and Operation of a Legionary Fortress

Logistical and Engineering Aspects

by D J P Mason PhD, FSA, MIFA

The installation of a garrison of 6,000 men accompanied by several thousand non-combatants and a very considerable number of pack and draught animals required a great deal of forward planning and logistical support. This was something at which the Roman army excelled, but it is only when one seriously contemplates the quantities of materials needed, as well as the effort required to bring them to the place of use, that the true scale of the task involved in building a legionary fortress becomes clear. This exercise does carry connotations of the 'anorak' or 'train-spotter' pastime but it is nonetheless extremely worthwhile in realising the magnificent achievements of which the Roman army was capable on a regular basis.

A secure supply of food for both men and animals was obviously the primary need but this is not an area that will be covered in this paper. That subject has been discussed extensively in print in recent years and so here, instead, we will concentrate on the logistical aspects of the raw and manufactured materials required for the actual construction of the fortress, their production and transportation to site. Also explored will be those features of the infrastructure needed to make the fortress function efficiently, where 6,000 men could live at close quarters in a controlled and healthy environment. The results of calculations made in preparation for this paper are set out in the tables below, and they make the point more than adequately. It remains to preface them with some observations of a more general nature and to highlight the most thought-provoking results of those calculations.

Vast amounts of timber had to be stockpiled before work began and a steady and reliable supply maintained thereafter so that progress would not be interrupted by a shortage of this most essential of materials (Table VIII.1). Before work started on the building of the fortress, however, the accommodation to house the workforce had to be erected — a not inconsiderable enterprise in its own right as the construction party probably numbered 2–3000 men. All this timber had to be felled, roughly shaped and transported to the fortress, where it was cut up into the required lengths and sizes. Wood was also needed for fuel, not so much for keeping warm in winter as for feeding the large number of kilns, furnaces and other industrial facilities needed to manufacture the wide range of building materials required: hundreds of tonnes of lime were needed to produce mortar and concrete, thousands of everyday items such as iron nails and bronze fittings, and hundreds of thousands of bricks and tiles. Excavations over the years have yielded valuable informa-

Table VIII.1 Flavian fortress construction: timber requirements

	Worked timber (m³)	Uncut timber (m³)	Weight (tonnes)	Wagon loads (800 kg)
Barracks incl centurions' quarters	14,476	19,301	12,546	15,682
Rampart buildings	1 ,080	1,440	936	1,170
Senior officers' houses	1,200	1,600	1,040	1,300
Auxiliary barracks	1,365	1,820	1,182	1,479
Principia	850	1,133	737	921
Hospital	1,000	1,333	866	1,083
Praetorium	400	533	347	433
Other *retentura*	1,350	1,800	1,170	1,462
Store	300	400	259	325
Workshops	500	666	433	542
Tabernae	1,425	1,900	1,235	1,543
Rampart	4,350	5,800	3,770	4,712
Gates & towers	625	833	541	677
Totals	**28,921**	**38,559**	**25, 062**	**31,329**
Construction camp/annexe	5,000	6,665	4,332	5,415
Amphitheatre	378	504	328	410
Mansio	500	667	434	542
Harbour works	1,200	1,600	1,040	1,300
Bridge	400	533	346	433
Scaffolding	100	133	86	108
Totals	**36,449**	**48,661**	**31, 628**	**39, 537**

Woodland felled to provide 31,628 tonnes of timber:
    744 ha (yield = 42.5 tonnes per ha)
    372 ha (yield = 85 tonnes per ha)
    197 ha (yield = 127.5 tonnes per ha)

tion about the size and spacing of the main vertical wall timbers in a variety of buildings within and without the early fortress, while general studies of Roman timber buildings undertaken in recent years provide a useful guide for estimating average volumes of timber needed for various forms of superstructure.

Thus, it can be calculated that over 14,000 m³ of worked timber would have been needed simply to construct the barracks, while the total for the fortress as a whole, including the vital extramural facilities such as the amphitheatre and the harbour works, comes to over 36,000 m³. This last figure equates to at least 39,000 wagonloads, assuming a carrying capacity of 800 kg, which demonstrates the transportation logistics involved and the requirement for a very sizeable fleet of wagons and a large number of draught animals. The sandstone ridge where the fortress was to be built probably had only a light tree cover, although the heavier clay land to the south and east may have been more densely forested. Yet there is evidence which indicates that even these areas had apparently already been subjected to significant clearance well before the advent of Rome, and so timber for the construction of the fortress probably had to be brought from some distance. The yield of usable timber per hectare must have varied widely and it is quite likely that several square kilometres were deforested to provide the timber needed. Had one been required in those days, it is doubtful if the environmental impact assessment would have proved favourable!

A few of the fortress buildings, principally the bath buildings, were built of masonry and concrete right from the beginning. Building stone was readily available from the rock outcrops in the close vicinity of the fortress, especially where the Dee had carved its way through the ridge to the south. Sand and clay were also to hand in vast quantities, while the cobbles which were used as aggregate in the concrete foundations of Flavian buildings could be picked up from the banks of the river. While only a few buildings were constructed in stone in this period, the quantities of materials involved were still very considerable, as is demonstrated by Table VIII.2 which lists those required for the main fortress baths. Over 400,000 blocks of stone were needed for the wall facing alone, and while it might have been possible to obtain some of this from the rock excavated to form the foundation trenches and hypocaust basements, the rest had to be transported by ox-drawn wagon up the steep slope of what is now Lower Bridge Street. With its extensive underfloor heating systems, this building required an enormous number of bricks — over 70,000 of the type 1 Roman foot square — as well as the vast quantity of tiles — 33,000 *tegulae* and 40,000 *imbrices* — needed to cover the roof. In all, the construction of this building consumed approximately 1,670 tonnes of brick and tile, including the 60 tonnes (200,000) of very small bricks employed in the herringbone-patterned flooring of the cold plunge baths. There was also about 1,460 m² of mosaic flooring composed of just over 3 million individually manufactured *tesserae*. Obviously water was the most important commodity in a bath building and the means of storing it and conveying it to where it was needed within this vast building consumed large amounts of another material — lead. Several hundred metres of pipework would have been necessary, while the two large reservoirs at the south end of the complex would have been lined with sheet lead. This equates to something like 75 tonnes of lead, or nearly 1,000 ingots of the 80 kg type which have been found at Chester (Ill VIII.1).

Table VIII.2 Flavian baths construction: material requirements

	Quantity (m³)	Weight (tonnes)	Wagonloads (800 kg)
Rock excavated	7, 000	17,500	21,875
Facing stones	418,600	7,500	9,375
Mortar	2,200	4,400	5,500
Concrete	1,350	2,700	3,375
Tile and brick			
Roof tiles			
Tegulae	33,176	376.5	471
Imbrices	40,001	127.2	159
Hypocaust pillars and suspended floors			
Pedales	70,000	339.2	424
Sesquipedales	2,800	62.8	78
Bipedales	2,200	65.1	81
Wall and vault lining			
Flue tiles	54,736	645	807
Flooring			
Opus spiccatum	200,000	60	75
Tesserae	3,057,175	9.8	12
Lead Distribution pipes			
Duodenaria and centenaria	39.6	50	
Reservoir linings	34.6	43	
Total = 927 ingots @ 80 kg ea			
Totals	**33,859.8**	**42, 325**	

Ill VIII.1 Lead ingot typical of those found at Chester.
(Copyright Chester City Council, Grosvenor Museum)

The reference to metals reminds us that some of the materials needed for the construction of the fortress were not available locally and had to be imported from the surrounding hinterland, sometimes entailing the transportation of bulky and/or weighty items over many kilometres. Extending the last calculation to the fortress as a whole, which we know had an internal distribution system using lead mains averaging 60 mm in diameter (although that serving the main baths may have been nearly three times this size), it is probable that the overall requirement was for 4–5,000 ingots of the type just mentioned. The lead ore or galena was mined in that part of Flintshire stretching from Talargoch, near Prestatyn, in the north to Minera, near Wrexham, in the south where it occurs in veins close to the surface. The beginning of imperial, as opposed to private, exploitation of these deposits is dated to AD 74 by the earliest surviving ingots, and this was presumably associated with preparations for the building of the fortress at Chester. The main refining centre from c AD 90 lay at Pentre Ffwrndan near Flint, and it is likely that an earlier facility lies nearby awaiting discovery. The ingots would have been transported to Chester by ship, and indeed one such was found in association with the remains of an early jetty beneath the Roodee.

Limestone, or rather its derivative lime, was also vital for the production of the thousands of tonnes of mortar and concrete needed for the construction of the various bath buildings in and around the primary fortress and the few other structures built of masonry in this period. The main baths would have needed around 3,500 cubic metres of mortar and concrete, and if we follow Vitruvius' recommended proportion of sand to lime of 2:1 then about 1,170 m³ of lime would have been needed for this building alone and probably around 4,000 m³ in total, which roughly equates to 4,800 tonnes. The main area of limestone in the region is more or less coincident with that containing the lead deposits and, in its reduced form, it too may have been transported to the fortress by sea rather than overland. This may also have been true of any exploitation of the iron and copper deposits lying further to the west. Right from its earliest days, therefore, it can be seen that the fortress drew upon the resources of an extensive hinterland. Some of this would have lain within the boundary of the *prata* or *territorium legionis*, the area under the direct control of the military, while the more outlying facilities came within the compass of its 'command area'.

Quite apart from water, the consumption of natural resources did not of course stop with the completion of the building of the fortress. Significant quantities of timber were required for everyday activities like cooking and heating, general building repairs, the manufacture of items spanning everything from writing tablets all the way through to furniture and vehicles, as well as fuel to keep the voracious furnaces of the bath buildings satisfied. In order to minimise the distances from which timber had to be brought, and also to ensure the quality of the timber, the military authorities would surely have practised some form of woodland management. The exploitation of metal ores would have continued, as would that of the extremely valuable salt deposits in central Cheshire.

There were, of course, times when the scale of consumption rocketed, most particularly when the fortress underwent one of its periodic reconstructions. Probably the best illustration of this is the renovation which took place in the second and third decades of the third century when every building inside the fortress was reconstructed, many from ground level, and when for the first time every building plot was fully utilised. The figures for the amount of building stone required (Table VIII.3) are quite astounding. Even making a 50% reduction of the total to allow for reusable stone in those cases where the earlier building was also constructed of masonry, the overall total still comes out at over 300,000 tonnes. Equally staggering is the 378,000 wagonloads which this represents. If the defences are included as well, then these figures increase to 359,000 and 448,000 respectively. One can now begin to see why the dating evidence associated with this event suggests some buildings were rebuilt *c* 220 and others *c* 230 or even later: it was simply that the logistics meant that it had to be a long drawn-out process.

While some of the earlier building stone would have been reusable this is most unlikely to have been the case with tile (Tables VIII.4, 5). Many of the earlier tiles would have become brittle and fragmented with age, while even the more robust examples are unlikely to have survived the dismantling process. One feels fairly certain therefore that most of the tile employed on the new Severan buildings was itself of recent manufacture. The plans of many buildings are known and the general form of the remainder can be estimated with reasonable confidence, and from this the size and form of their roof structures can be extrapolated. Allowing for breakages, the total number of *tegulae* and *imbrices* comes out at 930,000 and 1,156,000 respectively. Upwards of 70,000 antefixes might also have been required. The heating systems of the bath buildings were also included in the rebuilding programme, and although many of the bricks used for the hypocaust pillars would have been salvageable, those used for the underpinning of the concrete floors above them,

Table VIII.3 Severan fortress reconstruction: stone requirements

	Quantity (m3)	Weight (tonnes)	Wagonloads (800 kg)
Barracks	49,650	124,125	155,155
Rampart buildings*	4,288	10,720	13,400
Building behind HQ*	4,945	12,362	15,453
Granaries (x4)*	2,401	6,002	7,503
Granaries (x2)**	1,200	3,000	3,750
*Principia**	8,832	22,080	27,600
Elliptical Building**	7,450	18,625	23,280
Baths south of Elliptical Building*	510	1,275	1,594
Tabernae north of Elliptical Building*	671	1,677	2,096
Building north of Elliptical Building *insula***	2,808	7,020	8,775
Building/s in equivalent *insula* in east *latera praetorii***	2,808	7,020	8,775
Other buildings in *latera praetorii**	3,500	8,750	10,938
*Praetorium**	5,000	12,500	15,625
Main workshops*	2,246	5,615	7,019
Store*	2,500	6,250	7,813
Hospital*	3,500	8,750	10,938
Tribunes' houses*	7,500	18,750	23,438
Building/s opposite baths**	4,000	10,000	12,500
Other buildings in *praetentura***	3,500	8,750	10, 938
Other *tabernae**	3,575	8,937	11,170
Gates and towers	4,768	11,920	14,900
Totals	**125,652**	**314,128**	**392,660**

*   Earlier stone building completely reconstructed

**   New building

Table VIII.4 Severan fortress reconstruction: roof tile requirements

	Tegulae	Imbrices	Antefixes	Weight (tonnes)
Barracks*	377,664	446,205	27,486	5,758.33
Rampart buildings*	42,560	50,160	4,180	640.26
*Principia**	34,102	41,385	2,834	524.02
Building at rear of *principia**	53,578	65,466	3,484	823.17
Granaries* (6)	31,760	37,908	1,957	484.92
Elliptical Building (Laconian system for main range)*	6,536	43,035	1,570	214. 40
Building N of Elliptical Building*	7,680	9,508	771	118.83
Equivalent building in east *latera praetorii***	7,680	9,508	771	118.83
Store, east *latera praetorii***	17,940	22,020	1,160	275.91
Building N of *praetorium***	16,146	19,800	1,044	248.29
Main workshops*	24,288	30,008	1,898	374.74
Tribunes' etc houses**	50,416	63,824	5,528	785. 29
*Praetorium***	25,200	31,500	2,000	390.02
Other buildings in east *praetentura***	24,528	28,780	2,144	373.92
Hospital**	36,628	47,098	1,446	568.75
Remainder west *praetentura***	6,132	7,195	436	93.32
Remainder of *retentura***	12,264	14,390	872	186.64
*Tabernae**	60,780	74,926	4,050	936. 09
Gates and towers*	13,360	15,820	1,236	204.23
Major baths*	33,176	40,001	1,800	507.43
Minor baths*	2,364	3,064	100	36. 79
Totals incl 5% for breakages	**929,021**	**1,156,681**	**70,105**	**14,377.90**

*   Building form known

**   Building form estimated

Table VIII.5 Severan fortress reconstruction: other tile requirements

	Pedales	Solid brick Sesquipedales	Bipedales	Box-tile (double)	Weight (tonnes)
Major baths*	70,000	2,800	2,200	54,736	1,112.48
Minor baths*	3,200	236	183	1,600	44.74
Other hot bath suites and hypocausts**	12,000	1,000	800	1,600	121.68
Totals incl 5% for breakages	**89,460**	**4,237**	**3,342**	**60,832**	**1,342.84**

Total weight of brick and tile = 15,690.75 tonnes

= *c* 19,613 wagonloads @ 800 kg capacity

= 314 bargeloads @ 50 tonne capacity

*   – Building form known

**   – Building form estimated

Notes

1   Considerable amounts also required for official extramural structures such as bath-buildings and the *mansio*.

2   Broken brick and tile could be used as aggregate in, for example, concrete floors, road surfaces etc

3   High percentage of solid brick probably available for re-use

which were also replaced, would not. The hollow box tiles used for lining the walls in these buildings would also have had to be renewed. In addition, more buildings than ever before, especially the residences of junior officers and centurions, were equipped with hypocausts. In total, somewhere around 15,000 tonnes of brick and tile were needed for the rebuilding programme of the early to mid-third century, and this figure does not include the official buildings in the extramural area which are also likely to have been refurbished at this time: buildings such as the major baths complex near the present Water Gate and the *mansio* south of the fortress.

As far as we know, all of this brick and tile was produced in the legion's works depot at Holt and would undoubtedly have been transported the 12 km down river to the fortress by barge. On the assumption that the average load for a barge was 50 tonnes, this would have taken 300 barge-loads. Whether unloaded at a quay in the main harbour at the Roodee or at one located on the riverbank somewhere below the amphitheatre, there still remained the considerable task of moving this material up a steep slope to the fortress. The rebuilding programme would have been impossible without thousands of tonnes of lime and this, too, would have been transported by water, in this case by sea from one or more ports (Prestatyn and/or Flint) on the coast of north-east Wales. These two commodities demonstrate, if demonstration were needed, both the vital role played by water transport in supplying the garrison and the importance of Chester's possession of a decent harbour. This was true at all times, of course, not just during periodic rebuildings. Various types of pottery, glassware and other manufactured goods were imported by sea from abroad, along with wine and olive oil. Given the vast quantities of grain required, the bulk of this, too, was probably brought by ship from the south of the province, or even from other provinces as is known to have happened at both Caerleon and York.

The most important natural resource for any military or civilian community in the ancient world was a reliable and secure supply of good quality water, and for the Romans, whose lavish bathing facilities were a place for socialising and relaxation as much for cleansing and exercise, the supply also had to be copious. The remains of the civil engineering works carried out by the Romans to guarantee their water supplies constitute some of the most impressive monuments to have survived from the classical world. The mention of aqueducts usually conjures up images of tall arched masonry structures striding across the countryside and spanning steep-sided river valleys. Where the local geology and hydro-logy permitted, however, Roman aqueducts took a different form. The most common alternative was an underground pipeline, and such was the case at Chester. Before describ-ing Chester's aqueduct in detail, it must be remembered that Roman water-supply systems were generally based on the principle of continuous flow. Taps and stopcocks certainly existed but they could not cope with the enormous pressures that their modern counter-parts can endure, and so when the supply was shut off at one point there was usually at least one other part of the system to which it could be diverted and continue to flow unchecked. This may seem wasteful to modern eyes, but a great excess of supply over demand was the only way of ensuring a constant flow of fresh water in an age without chemical treatments, while the continuously overflowing fountains, water troughs and other outlets provided a volume of water sufficient to flush and purge the drainage system. This explains why, as it has been calculated, the typical Roman household consumed in one day the amount of water that a modern household would use over two months. Because there were certain times of the day and night when there was a rapid increase in demand, for example when the pools in the baths were drained and replenished, Roman supply systems also incorporated a considerable storage capability in the form of reservoirs — *castella aquae*. The principal reservoir, the *castellum divisorium*, was sited at the point where the aqueduct entered the town or fortress and, as one might guess from its name, it was built with mechanisms which allowed the amount of water supplied to different areas to be regulated.

The source of Deva's water supply lay 2 km east of the fortress, in the area now occupied by the suburb of Boughton, where a water-bearing layer of sand emerged from between two layers of boulder clay (Ill VIII.2). Although long since covered by housing develop-ments, this was once a major source of fresh water, and the scale of its output can be judged by the fact that when this aquifer was cut through by an excavation for a railway cutting in 1885 it flooded Chester station to a depth of three feet. The remains of the Roman waterworks structure were found in 1821, together with an altar dedicated by the Twentieth Legion to the 'nymphs and fountains'. This spot lies at a height of 27 m OD, and the fall to 21.5 m OD at the point where the aqueduct entered the fortress at the east gate

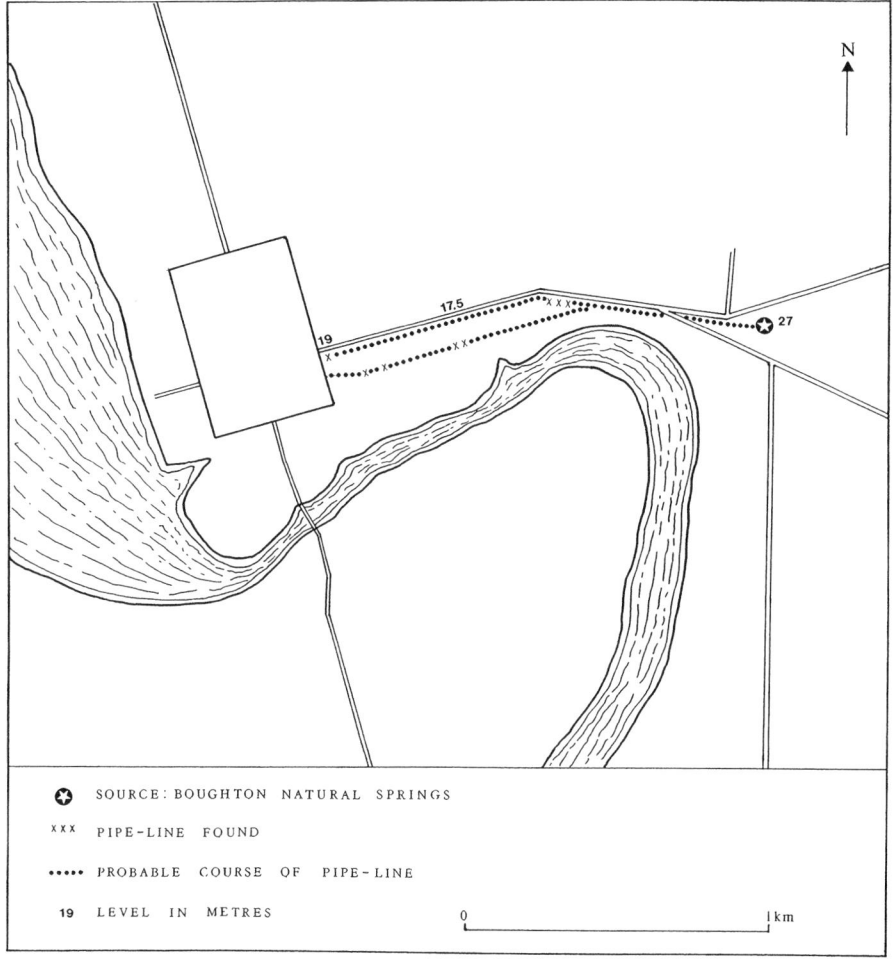

Ill VIII.2 Source of fortress water supply and course of aqueduct: map. (Scale 1/25 000)

was more than sufficient for a gravity feed system. However, in order that water could be supplied to all areas of the fortress, the water level in the *castellum divisorium* must have been raised to a height about 1 m higher than that of the highest point of the interior (the north end), that is about 31.5 m OD. This means that not only would the water reservoir beside the east gate have been quite an impressive structure, with a height in excess of 10 m, but also the water must have been raised artificially at the point where it entered the system. This would have been perfectly feasible as the land around the source at Boughton rises to a height greater than that of the high point of the fortress. Most probably, the structure found in 1821 was a reservoir, served by adits radiating out into the surrounding sand stratum, where the water was raised to a height of about 32 m OD. The water was conveyed to the fortress by means of a pipeline formed of interlocking terracotta pipes (averaging 700 mm in length with a bore of 130 mm) laid in the base of a 2-m-deep trench which was then backfilled with solid clay so as to contain the pressure at the joints. Given the weight of the clay, this must have been a fairly tricky operation, and one imagines the successful employment of this technique must have entailed a considerable degree of previous experimentation. The pipe ran along the south side of the road leading to the east gate of the fortress, where it would have risen up the side of the *castellum divisorium*. There was in fact a second identical pipeline running almost parallel with the first but some 100 m further to the south. This may have been a dedicated pipeline serving the main baths in the forward area of the fortress, in whose general direction it was heading. However, it soon passed out of use — if it was ever actually completed — and it would appear that one pipeline was sufficient for the entire needs of the fortress.

Lengths of water main found at various points within the fortress show that the internal distribution system consisted of lead pipes with a bore of *c* 60mm, which is close to the standard Roman pipe size known as the *duodenaria*. That serving the baths, however, may have been considerably larger, perhaps of *centenaria* size (bore of *c* 200 mm), and there may have been a pipe of similar size running beneath the *via principalis* on its way to the extensive extramural baths complex situated in the vicinity of the Water Gate. The location of known and assumed components of the distribution system are shown on Ill VIII.3. These pipes, or smaller bore take-offs from them, would have fed drinking fountains, water troughs, and minor reservoirs distributed throughout the fortress, as well as individual buildings. Based on the number, type and known dimensions of the facilities in several of the bath buildings, the likely capacities and consumption rates of the other major water-consuming buildings, and the probable needs of the garrison for water used for drinking and cooking, an estimate can be made of the minimum water requirement of the fortress and the official extramural buildings per 24-hour cycle. As can be seen from Table VIII.6 below, the total comes to nearly 2.4 million litres. Calculations suggest that even one pipeline of the size known, operating with fairly modest head of 1 m, could have supplied the fortresss with *c* 3 million litres per 24 hours. Given that the distribution system as well as some of the buildings themselves incorporated a significant storage capacity, it appears that just one pipeline could have satisfied the entire needs of both the fortress and the official extramural buildings.

Disposing of all this water was equally important and, as one might expect, this was achieved with equal efficiency and economy. In this, the Roman engineers were helped by the natural topography of the fortress site; or perhaps a consideration of the drainage requirements was one of the reasons behind the choice of this precise site. Overall, the site sloped from north to south while the 'hog's back' shape of the ridge, with the longitudinal axis of the fortress positioned along the 'spine', meant that the ground fell away to the east and west of its centre line — all facts which greatly facilitated a speedy and thus effective rate of flow in the drainage system (Ill VIII.4). A large drain ran beneath many of the secondary streets, into which the lesser drains as well as the simple, open eavesdrip gulleys along the edges of the streets disgorged. Although opportunities to test the point have not arisen so far, it is probable that there were two such sewers beneath the major streets such as the *via principalis* and *via praetoria*. All of the above flowed into an intercepting sewer which ran around the entire fortress beneath and beside the inner edge of the *intervallum* road. This had its principal outfalls beneath the south-east and south-west angles of the

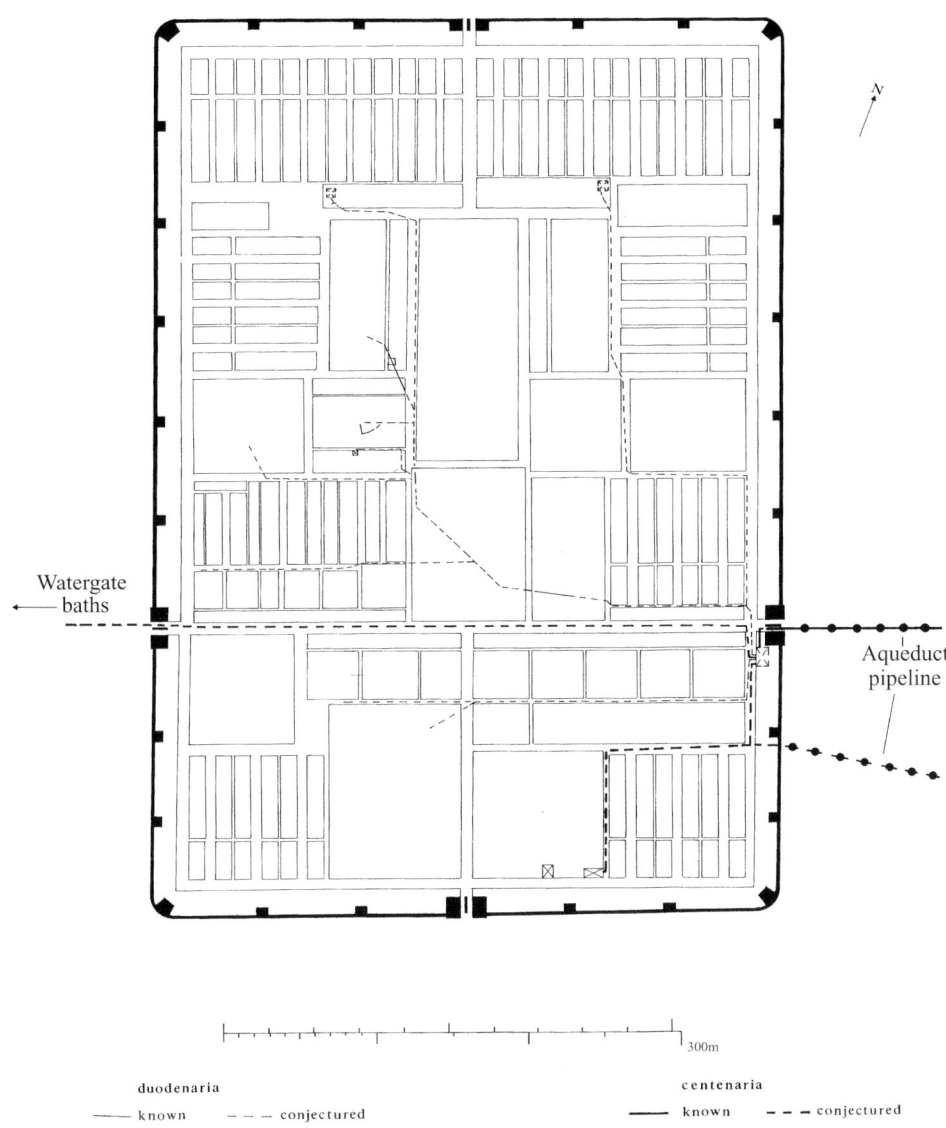

Watergate
baths

Aqueduct
pipeline

300m

duodenaria

—— known — – – conjectured

centenaria

—— known — – – conjectured

Ill VIII.3 Water distribution system within fortress: plan. (Scale 1/5000)

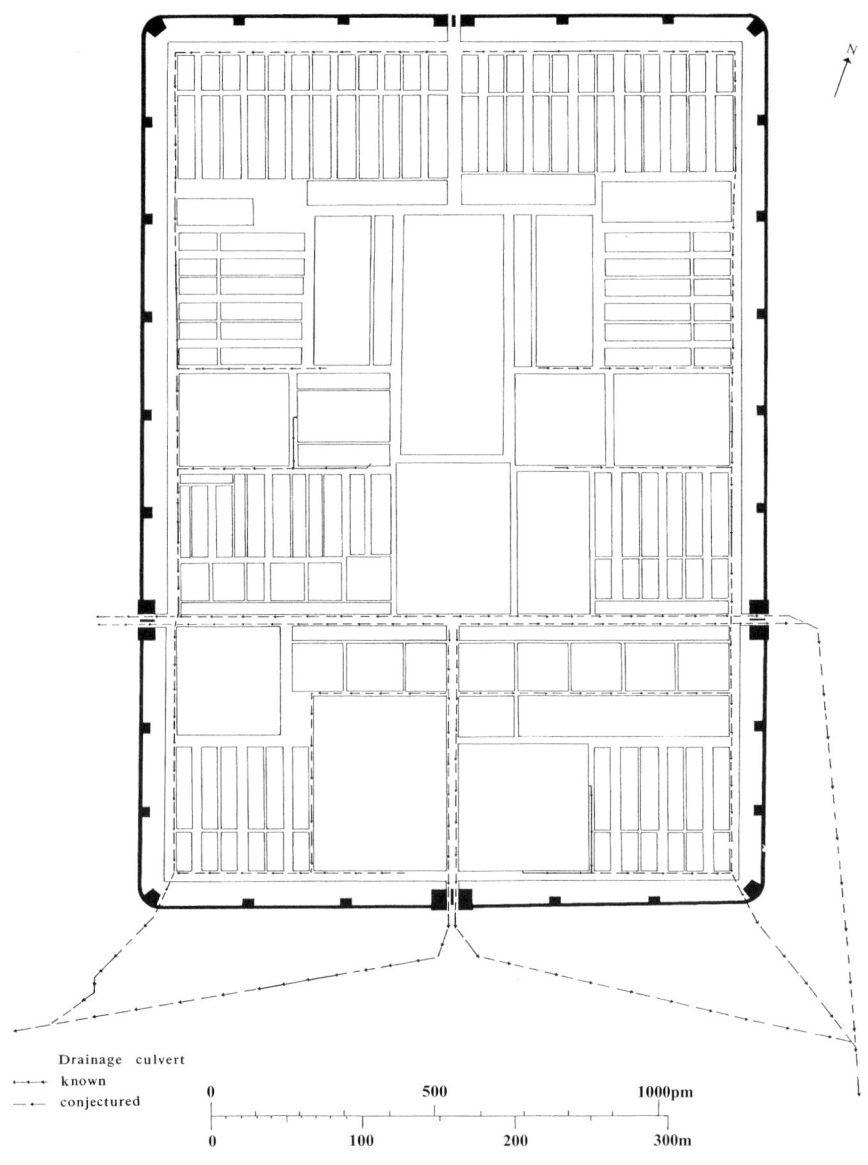

III VIII.4 Fortress drainage system: plan. (Scale 1/5000)

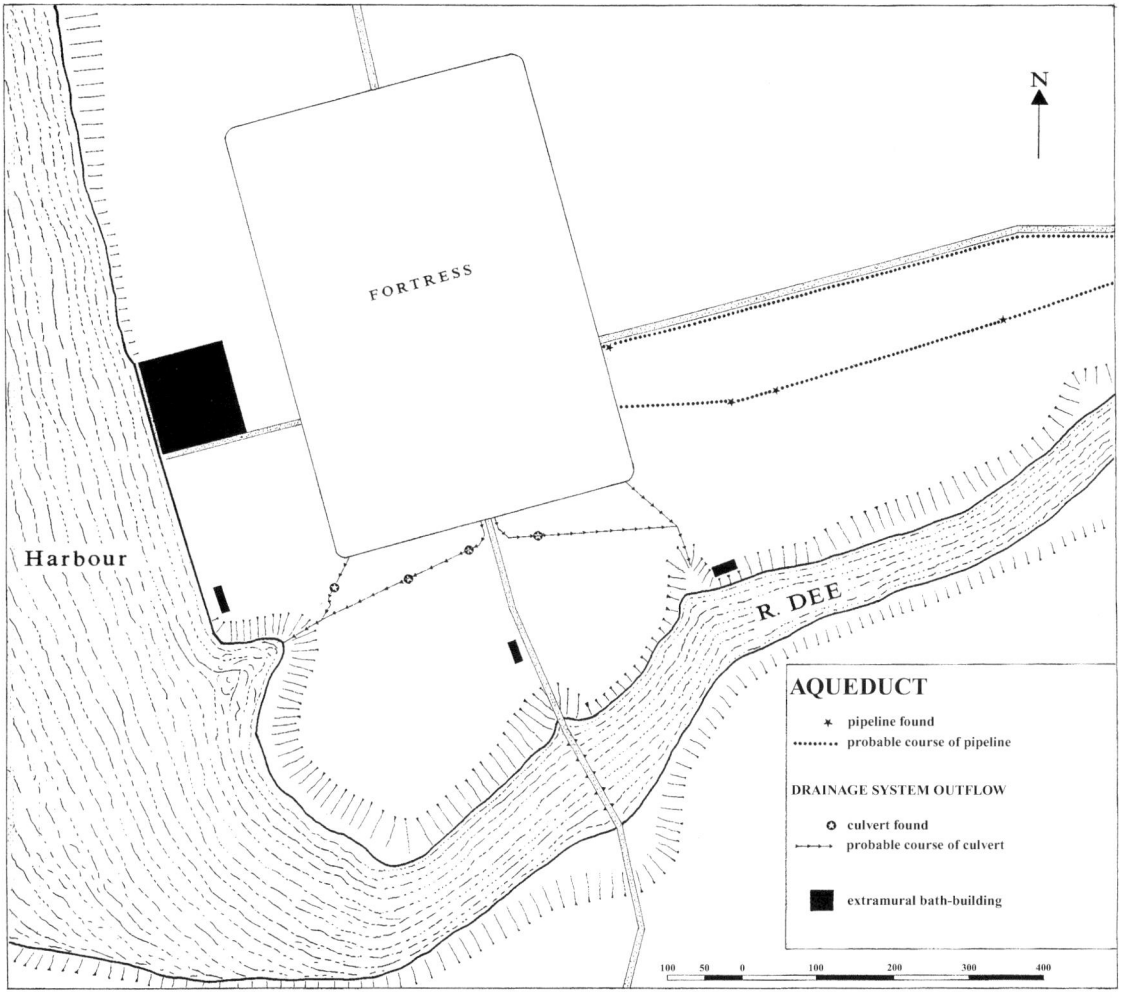

Ill VIII.5 Main outflows of fortress drainage system: plan. (Scale 1/10 000)

fortress where, some distance outside the defences, each was joined by one of the sewers which exited from the south gate (*see* Ill VIII.5). Ultimately, these outfalls debouched into the natural declivities in the area of Souter's Lane and Nun's Road respectively.

Bath buildings have featured prominently in the foregoing and it is logical that the concluding part of this paper should concentrate on the most extensively explored and, in the light of recent research, the best understood of Chester's examples — the fortress baths. The north end of this complex was uncovered during building works in 1863 and, fortunately, some of the founding members of the Society were on hand to record its remains. An extensive report written by Dr Thomas Brushfield was published in volume 3 of the old series of the Society's *Journal* and included what must be some of the earliest photographs taken for the purposes of archaeological recording (*see* Ills VIII.6 and 7). Further remains were uncovered in the opening decades of the twentieth century and then,

III VIII.6 Remains of exercise hall of fortress baths exposed by clearance of Feathers Hotel, Bridge Street, 1863. The bases of the two rows of columns of the *basilica* are clearly visible.
(*J Chester Archaeol Soc* old ser **3**, 1885, frontispiece)

in 1963, almost the whole of the eastern half of this enormous building was uncovered and then rapidly destroyed with only the minimum of archaeological recording to make way for the construction of a shopping precinct. Quite apart from the wealth of irreplaceable archaeological information that was lost forever, the City missed out on the opportunity to display some of the most impressive Roman remains ever found in Chester, including rooms with completely intact hypocaust heating systems and walls still standing to a height of nearly 4 m. All was not completely lost, however, because Dennis Petch (then Curator of the Grosvenor Museum), despite the very trying circumstances, was able to retrieve a considerable amount of information which, together with the details recorded earlier, the speaker was recently commissioned by Chester Archaeology to analyse and work up into a comprehensive report. This process is very close to completion and it is intended that the report will be published in 2002.

The fortress baths complex was approximately 84 m square overall and consisted of four principal elements (Ill VIII.8). Across the north end was a large covered exercise hall of basilical form 12 m wide and more than 50 m long. Attached to the western half of its south side was a suite of three hypocausted rooms which provided a bathing regime of dry heat like a modern sauna. East of these was the first of three large, barrel-vaulted halls, each measuring 12 m across and a minimum of 20 m in length arranged in a north–south progression of increasing temperature — *frigidarium*, *tepidarium* and *caldarium*. The atmosphere in this part of the baths was very humid, much like that in Turkish baths. A feature of both the *frigidarium* and the *caldarium* was the provision of semi-circular recesses containing free-standing communal washbasins (*labra*) as well as large bathing

Ill VIII.7 Close-up of column base and fallen column drum
found on Feathers Hotel site 1863.
(*J Chester Archaeol Soc* old ser **3**, 1885, facing 56)

pools, cold *piscinae* in the former and hot (*alvei*) in the latter. The pool at the west end of the *caldarium* was particularly large, about 11 m across, and was housed in an apsidal bay which projected from the main body of the building in order to catch the maximum amount of sunlight. Centrally positioned against the south wall of the *caldarium* lay the main furnace house or *praefurnium* containing two large furnaces. These supplied heat to the *caldarium* hypocaust, which then passed into the *tepidarium* beyond through arched flues in the base of the party wall, and also heated boilers which supplied hot water to the pool and *labra* ranged along its south side. Auxiliary *praefurnia* to either side of the main furnace house heated the pools located at the ends of the *caldarium*. In case it was necessary to boost the temperature in the neighbouring *tepidarium*, this was provided with two smaller *praefurnia*, one in the middle of each of its shorter sides. The main water reservoir (*castellum aquae*) was sited in the south-east comer of the complex. Its foundation consisted of a massive concrete base 11 m long, 7 m wide and 1.2 m thick (Ill VIII.9). The fact that this was surmounted by fifteen substantial blocks of sandstone arranged in three

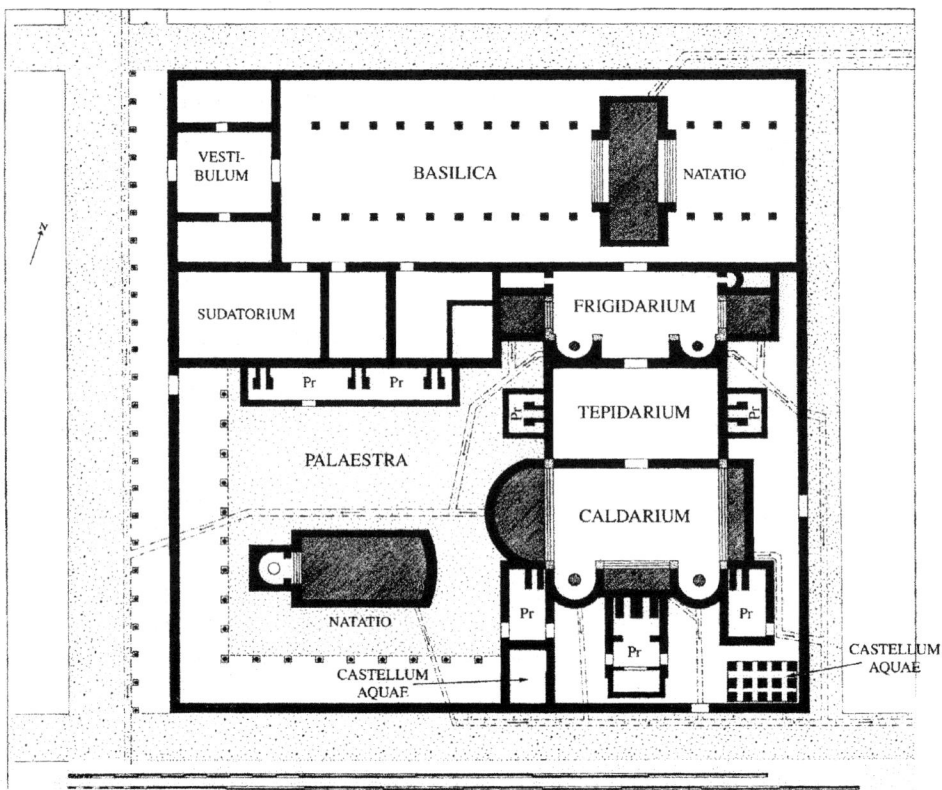

III VIII.8 Fortress baths as built *c* AD 75: plan. (Scale 1/10 000)

rows of five indicates that the reservoir tank was raised off the ground, probably taking the form of a wood and iron frame clad with lead sheeting supported by fifteen stone pillars. The other *castellum* lay to the west beside the fourth element of the complex, the open air exercise yard or *palaestra* whose principal feature was a swimming bath (*natatio*).

The operation and maintenance of such a massive, comparatively sophisticated and intensively used complex must have been a major enterprise. Including those which heated the dry air sweat baths, there were nine furnaces, and keeping these supplied with fuel very probably required at least 2,000 tonnes of wood per annum. The quantity of water consumed was even more prodigious. The large fountains-cum-washbasins were supplied with running water throughout the day, as probably were the fountains which fed the large cold swimming baths in the *basilica*, the *frigidarium* and the *palaestra*. Without chemicals to treat the water and because of the extensive use of oils as part of the Roman bathing process, the pools had to be drained and replenished every day after dusk. This would have entailed the furnaces serving the *caldarium* providing a minimum of 63,000 litres of hot water by the following morning and the re-supply of the cold baths with approximately 555,000 litres. It was only after the last customers of the day had vacated the building that the real work began. Taking into account the supply to fountains and similar facilities

III VIII.9 Concrete bases which supported the main reservoir for the fortress baths, photographed during destruction in 1963 to make way for the Grosvenor Shopping Centre.
(Copyright Chester City Council)

during the day, it is estimated the fortress baths consumed something of the order of 850,000 litres of water in each 24-hour cycle (Tables VIII.6–7).

As with many Roman buildings one can detect in their dimensions the use, or apparent use, of standard units of measurement. Thus, the columns in the exercise hall were spaced at intervals, centre to centre, of 12 Roman feet (the Roman foot here taken to be the *pes Monetalis* (pM), corresponding to 295 mm), while the distance between the two rows of columns was 11.80 m or 40 pM and the width of each aisle 5.95 m = 20 pM. The suite of dry heat rooms was also 11.80 m or 40pM wide, while the core area of all three halls in the main bathing suite measured 11.80 x 20.65 m = 40 x 70 pM.

Legionary bath buildings, both those built in fortresses and in the veteran settlements (*coloniae*), were the forerunners of the great imperial baths constructed in Rome from the late first century onwards — structures such as the Baths of Titus, the Baths of Trajan and so on. Comparing the plans of bath buildings belonging to Claudian, Neronian and Flavian legionary fortresses and *coloniae*, it is clear that the design of these complexes, with their sophisticated heating and water-supply systems and pioneering use of large-scale concrete roof vaulting, underwent rapid development during the middle decades of the first century. In early examples in the series, such as the Claudian baths at Vindonissa, the *frigidarium* was not yet fully integrated but had become so by the time the legionary baths at Exeter were built *c* AD 55. The development of the covered exercise hall also illustrates the evolution of these buildings. A *basilica* was not provided in the legionary baths at Vindonissa nor in the contemporary colonial baths at Augusta Raurica. It was also absent

Table VIII.6 Minimum fortress and official building water requirement per 24-hour cycle

	Facility	Quantity (litres)
Hygiene	Fortress baths	850,000
	Elliptical Building baths	80,000
	Watergate baths	850,000
	Amphitheatre baths	100,000
	Mansio baths	100,000
	Blackfriars baths	80,000
	Hospital	20,000
Industrial	Workshops	40,000
Refreshment and cooking	Fountains and troughs	15,000
Ornamental	Fountains (*Praetorium*, Elliptical Building etc)	100,000
Total		**2,370,000**

from the (probably early Flavian) extramural baths at Wroxeter, while at Caerleon, founded within a year or two of Chester, it appears to have been an afterthought. It was, however, clearly part of the original design for the Chester baths, which at present have the distinction of being the earliest legionary baths to have this facility as an integral feature. The possession of an exercise hall of basilical form subsequently became *de rigueur* for major bathing complexes both civil and military, as is demonstrated by the town baths at Wroxeter (Hadrianic), the legionary baths at Aquincum (Trajanic) and the colonial baths at Xanten (Trajanic). The Chester baths are also notable for their rare provision of a swimming bath within the *basilica*, a feature only found elsewhere in the legionary baths of Trajanic date at Aquincum, a fortress also built by Legion II *Adiutrix*, the initial garrison of the Chester fortress.

Despite the execrable conditions under which the 1960s investigations took place, some remarkable details of the construction techniques employed in the roof vaulting of the baths were recovered. In the *tepidarium*, the floor overlying the hypocaust was found to be intact in many places, and overlying it were the deposits which had accumulated in the period when the building had ceased to function as a working baths but was still standing. Over what had obviously been a very long period the floor became covered to a depth of about 400 mm by a layer of earth which, in addition to fragments of mortar and plaster which presumably originated from the decaying fabric of the bathing hall, also contained pieces of animal bone and a significant amount of charcoal. The inference would seem to be that the baths were occupied by 'squatters' for a substantial length of time in the sub-Roman period and possibly later. In the absence of scientific analysis of the deposits

Table VIII.7 Fortress baths: water requirement per 24-hour cycle

	Facility	Quantity (litres)
Hot		
Basilica	natatio	197,400
	fountain	55,000
Palaestra	natatio	302,400
	fountain	55,000
Frigidarium	piscinae	54,000
	labra	55,000
	latrine & drinking fountain	12,000
Total		**730,800**
Hot		
Caldarium	alveus (east)	23,100
	alveus (west)	23,100
	alveus (south)	20,064
	labra	55,000
Total		**121,264**
Grand total		**852,064**

overlying the floor it is obviously impossible to tell how long this form of occupation lasted, but it was clear that use of the building, or at least this part of it, was terminated by the collapse of a major portion of the roof structure which crashed down onto the earth covered floor (Ill VIII.10). This earth deposit cushioned the impact and thus prevented the disintegration of the components of the roof vaulting. At the top of the c 600-mm-thick layer of debris were the *tegulae* and *imbrices* of the external tile cladding. Below these were the remains of the main body of the roof, the concrete vault itself and below this again the shattered fragments of box tiles belonging to the inner, hollow lining of the vault. The latter was a continuation of the wall jacketing through which hot gases from the hypocaust were conducted. Thus, not only the floor but also the walls and the ceiling radiated heat. At one point within the mass of fragmented box tile were five or six lines of small, interlocking ceramic pipes, each one about the size of a milk bottle, bonded together with a rich lime plaster (Ill VIII.11). Known as *tubi fittili*, these were commonly employed in vault and dome construction in the later Roman period and there are many surviving examples of their use in fourth-century churches in northern Italy, especially those at Ravenna. The technique appears to have originated somewhat earlier in North Africa where they were used, principally in bath buildings, as a substitute for timber centring to form a continuous framework on which concrete vaults could be laid. The particularly fine

III VIII.10 Concrete floor of *tepidarium* of fortress baths with debris of collapsed roofing vault resting on dark sub-Roman dereliction layer; lines of *tubi fittili* clearly visible. (Copyright Chester City Council)

III VIII.11 Close-up of *tubi fittili*. (Copyright Chester City Council)

Ill VIII.12 Examples of *tubi fittili* in position used as inner lining of vault at Bulla Regia, Tunisia.
(Photo courtesy T J Strickland)

example shown here is the vault of the *frigidarium* in the baths at Bulla Regia in Tunisia (Ill VIII.12). In all these examples, however, the *tubuli* were used to form a continuous lining, whereas in the Chester baths by contrast they appear to have been employed in groups of five or six lines at intervals. It would seem , therefore, that they were used in the same way as the single lines of bricks or solid voussoirs incorporated in the vaults of other bath buildings, that is as ribs placed at intervals which, by dividing up the vault into compartments, made it both stronger and easier to construct. As *tubi fittili* of this form are not known to have been used before the middle of the second century the vault of which they formed part was probably erected during the extensive reconstruction of the fortress and its buildings which occurred in the second and third decades of the third century.

Further Reading

Bidwell, P T 1979   The legionary bath house and basilica and forum at Exeter. Exeter City Council

Brodribb, C 1987   Roman brick and tile. Gloucester: Alan Sutton

Burford, A 1960   Heavy transport in antiquity. *Econom Hist Rev* **13**, 1–18

Hanson, W S 1978   The organisation of Roman military timber supply. *Britannia* **9**, 293–305

Hodge, A T *et al* 1992   Roman aqueducts and water supply. London: Duckworth

Kendal, R 1996   Transport logistics associated with the building of Hadrian's Wall. *Britannia* **27**, 129–5

Landels, J G 1978   Engineering in the ancient world. London: Chatto & Windus

Nielsen, I 1990   *Thermae et balnea*. 2 vols. Aarhus U P

Shirley, E A M 1996   The building of the legionary fortress at Inchtuthil. *Britannia* **27**, 111–128

Wilson, R J A 1992   Terracotta vaulting tubes (*tubi fittili*): on their origin and distribution. *J Roman Archaeol* **5**, 97–129

Yegül, F 1992   Baths and bathing in classical antiquity. London: MIT Press

IX: Deva Victrix Restored

The Application of Computer 3-D Modelling Techniques in the Reconstruction of Roman Chester

by Julian Baum & D J Robinson BA, MPhil[1]

As the result of a chance meeting which took place several years ago between the authors of this paper, a conversation developed on the possibility of re-constructing all of the Roman buildings of Chester on a computer. It was agreed that Julian should start with a barrack block, on the assumption that this was the simplest and best understood of the structures which have been excavated to date. The success of these initial reconstructions persuaded us to carry on with what we have called 'The Chester Project', but now extending it to take advantage of the expertise of other specialists in the archaeology of Roman Chester, in particular Peter Carrington, David Mason and Tim Strickland.

Like many other built environments, Roman Chester saw many changes during its long history. The moment in time we have decided to represent in the Chester Project is the early third century. This may seem at first glance an unusually late date to choose for a major Roman site in Britain, but in fact it does reflect the archaeological evidence which indicates that this was the only period in its history when the fortress was fully manned and had its full complement of buildings.

The concept behind the project is twofold: firstly, of course, our aim is to provide a public face for the work of the archaeologists, but secondly, and equally important in our view, is to identify problems of understanding which are glossed over or obscured by the conventional black-and-white archaeological plans. After all, it is quite easy to present a plausible representation of a building if you do not have to explain where the doors are, how to get to the upper storey, or what holds the roof up. Our aim has been to be as accurate as we can; having said that there are many areas of speculation when it comes to three-dimensional reconstructions, and it is our intention to offer solutions, sometimes provocative, which will stimulate other archaeologists to debate the issues which we have raised. Hopefully this will provide a consensus view........!

Another use of computer graphics is to provide an approximate method of quantity surveying. The materials needed for the roof of a barrack block can serve as an example. By constructing one average roof tile and asking the computer to multiply it as many times

1   Julian Baum, Freelance Computer Artist; Dan Robinson, Keeper of Archaeology, Chester Museums

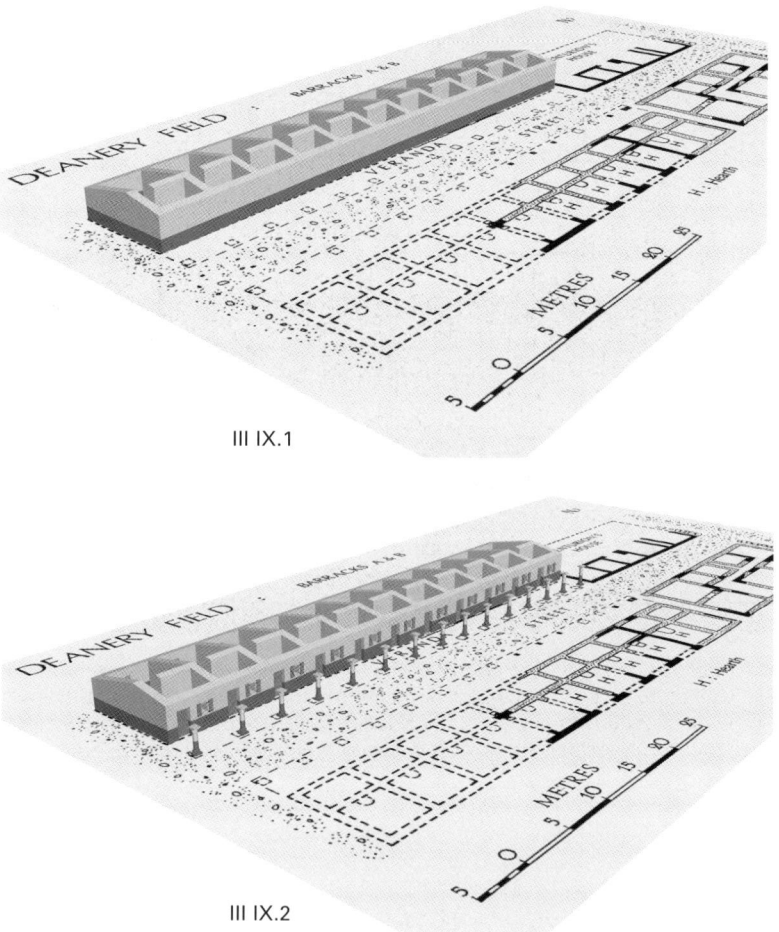

III IX.1

III IX.2

The reconstructed barrack building demonstrates its use of archaeological data, mostly from the Deanery Field excavations carried out by Professor Robert Newstead in the 1920s and 1930s. The published plan is the base, and in the case of a relatively simple structure like this it is used directly as a template to control the computer three-dimensional modelling of the barrack.

The barrack at this simple level of detail is made of extruded planes. In the case of basic evaluations like this, it can be presumed that the barrack maintains the same profile along its length. The profile is drawn as a two-dimensional template then extruded to the length of the original barrack. There is no real-world equivalent to this process, and in a similar manner blocks representing the volume of each *contubernium* are built, then subtracted from the solid barrack object, leaving space for the walls. Smaller blocks, matching presumed dimensions of doors and windows, are again subtracted from the main barrack object. The veranda columns are also constructed first as a two-dimensional template; the profile is then spun around an axis to produce a three-dimensional image. The profile can be derived from drawings of site finds, reconstruction drawings or from photos of column bases and capitals; in the last case the drum can then be extrapolated according to the type of column required.

Ill IX.3 This overview of the north-eastern corner of the fortress is provided to show how the use of a basic level of detail can be expanded, building on the known and extrapolated plan which has been developed from archaeological research. Once we can see the three-dimensional spacing of the structures we can get a clearer perception of the 'townscape' of the fortress.

as necessary to cover the roof, we can get a fair idea of how many might be needed for a single barrack. Once the principle is established this can be extended to any building. Since we know the weight of a single tile we could similarly calculate a total weight for a roof.

The figures we have produced for one of the Deanery Field barracks, in the north-east corner of the fortress, are:

Barrack block (*contubernia*)	3,360 *tegulae*	3,304 *imbrices*
Centurion's quarters	1,764 *tegulae*	1,708 *imbrices*
Total	**5,124 *tegulae***	**5,012 *imbrices***
Total number of tiles	**10,136**	

There were also, of course, antefixes, but their number is unknown. We are inclined to believe that they occurred only at ridge ends, and since Chester barrack blocks were built with the centurion's quarters as a separate unit there may have been four antefixes rather than two per block.

III IX.4

III IX.5

As an illustration of the sort of issue that may be thrown up by the reconstruction process, two versions of the centurion's quarters at the end of the barrack block are shown here. It is usually assumed that the roof structure for a barrack block was a single continuous surface; but at Chester we have a small alleyway between the centurions' quarters and the *contubernia*. Since we know that the difference in status between the centurion and the common soldier was considerable, is it not possible that the walls of the centurions' quarters were slightly higher to emphasise the difference? To demonstrate, we have included one image showing the regular roof level on a centurion's quarters and another version with a higher one; the archaeological evidence would support either. Computer reconstruction is a useful tool for testing such interpretations.

III IX.6 The most dramatic reconstruction so far is of the 'Elliptical Building' — an enigmatic grandiose structure at the heart of the fortress. Begun in the 70s of the first century it was abandoned before it had progressed beyond foundation level. Construction started again almost 160 years later and the building was finally completed to almost the original design, suggesting that the first-century plans must have survived in an office somewhere to resurface in the third century. The view shown here is the eastern side of the third-century building. The Elliptical Building in reality stood very close to the next building to the east, so that nobody in Roman times would have been able to stand back far enough to admire this magnificent façade.

Other calculations show that it would have been possible to assemble the complete legion in the cross hall of the *principia*, which perhaps indicates that this calculation influenced its size. The legion could also have been assembled in the courtyard outside.

The Chester Project is not formally funded and this has inevitably delayed progress; most of what has been achieved has been done in Julian's spare time. Advantage has been taken of the publication of reports on the Elliptical Building and that on the fortress bath house (both compiled by David Mason and published by Chester Archaeology) and the fortress defences (compiled by Charles LeQuesne and published by Chester Archaeology and Giffords) to add the reconstructions of these elements to the package of buildings which will ultimately be combined to make a total picture of Roman Chester.

Our ultimate aim is to create a complete virtual fortress, with the ability to 'walk' the streets and enter at least some of the buildings. The program will be accessible in the Grosvenor Museum in Chester, where a pilot version, using some basic elements from the project, is already running in the Newstead Gallery, and it should be possible to make the Chester Project available on CD for schools or the general public if there proves to be a market. Development work is also available on the web at www.chesterproject.co.uk.

Index